TOBACCO AND THE COLLECTOR

Also by Amoret and Christopher Scott

COLLECTING BYGONES

THE A TO Z OF ANTIQUE COLLECTING

TOBACCO
AND THE COLLECTOR

AMORET AND CHRISTOPHER SCOTT

Illustrated by
CÉCILE CURTIS

MAX PARRISH · LONDON

MAX PARRISH AND CO LTD
1–5 PORTPOOL LANE
LONDON EC 1

To K.M.E. and H.S.E. this book is
affectionately dedicated

Acknowledgements

Our grateful thanks are due to Messrs W. D. & H. O. Wills and to Ronson Products Ltd., for help in our researches; and to Joyce Finn for her great efforts in the preparation of the manuscript.

Contents

	A WORD ABOUT COLLECTING	11
1	THE STORY OF TOBACCO	13
2	PIPES	24
3	PIPE ACCESSORIES	44
4	TOBACCO JARS AND BOXES	59
5	STRIKING A LIGHT	72
6	MATCHBOX LABELS	99
7	SNUFF	109
8	TRADE SIGNS, TOKENS AND CARDS	126
9	DRESS AND FURNITURE	139
10	CIGARS	148
11	CIGARETTES	159
12	CIGARETTE CARDS	167
13	THE LAST PUFF	175
	AN ABBREVIATED BIBLIOGRAPHY	176
	INDEX	177

List of Plates

(between pp. 138 and 139)

A shop sign advertising the sale of snuff and tobacco

Lead tobacco box with Negro's head trade mark c. 1800; two bone match boxes c. 1880; straw-work match box with bone serrated end for striking matches c. 1850; ram's head match box for watch chain c. 1880.

Collection of tobaconists' business cards from eighteenth and nineteenth centuries

A word about collecting

This is not a book about antiques. It is a book about collecting. The fun of collecting depends to a very large degree on the limits one sets. There is nothing easier than collecting without limits, and nothing more pointless. If one decides to collect china, for example, and narrows the field down no further than that, one can buy until one's money runs out – which it will do very quickly – and then find one has amassed a hotchpotch of unrelated items that cannot possibly give any corporate pleasure or have any meaning as a group. The answer, of course, is to narrow one's aims down drastically – not to collect china, but let us say examples of scale-pattern Worcester. This will bring the fun of the hunt; the excitement of finding, very occasionally, what one is looking for; the pleasure of matching piece with piece; and the satisfaction of becoming, as one certainly will, an expert.

One of the difficulties of making a collection is cost. Even Worcester scale-pattern china is likely to make a considerable breach in one's resources. We have been conscious for some time that for would-be collectors of limited means, antiques are out. We stopped trying to collect them years ago. But we found several other fields which allow us to collect quite amazingly cheaply and with enormous pleasure. One of these fields has been the bygones of tobacco. There are still to be found in considerable quantities small objects, part of the paraphernalia of smokers and snuffers from the end of the sixteenth century almost to the present day. Some of them are in antique shops, particularly the handsome and expensive snuff boxes of the eighteenth century; but most of them are lying about in junk shops, often unrecognised for what they are. To take only one example from the following chapters, the development in Victorian times of the match, after hundreds of years of the flint-and-steel, produced within a period of about fifty years a succession of new improvements and a host of attractive containers – all of which disappeared when the safety match and the chip-board box came in.

We have written this book for the collector, but we make no apology for including not a little of the historical background. To us, it is knowing how the things we collect fit into the settings which produced them, that makes our collections the pleasure and the interest that they are.

1 . The Story of Tobacco

We have been smoking now for about four hundred years. In that time the story of tobacco has divided itself into some remarkable chapters, and has left behind it a wealth of small objects which are of interest to the collector. In the following pages we have brought together a representative selection of these, together with a few words in each case to fit them into the historical framework of the use of tobacco in its various forms. It follows that much of the history of smoking will appear piecemeal throughout the book, and for this reason we thought that it would be sensible, even at the risk of saying the same thing twice, to begin with a chronological account of the development of smoking, from the earliest times to the present day.

It is almost certain that tobacco-smoking, at least as a social habit, was unknown anywhere in the world much before the Christian era. The burning of incense as an offering to the gods was practised in Egypt three thousand years before that, however, and the basic roots of smoking certainly extend as far as this. But the tobacco plant was unknown in Egypt, and remained unknown until about 1600.

Neither the Greeks nor the Romans knew anything of tobacco, although one interesting preview of the events of sixteen centuries later is to be found in the writings of Pliny. He lived in the first century A.D., and devoted most of his life (which ended in the eruption of Vesuvius in A.D. 79) to a work on natural history in seventy-three volumes. Twelve of these were concerned with medicines derived from plants, and in one he recommends inhaling the smoke of burning coltsfoot through a reed as a cure for a cough. This must be one of the earliest signs of the pipe in Europe. It must certainly be the only occasion in history when smoking has been put forward as a cure for, rather than a cause of, coughing. The Greeks by this time had already been stupefying themselves for hundreds of years with the smoke of hemp-seed, scattered on red-hot stones; 'reefers' have a long pedigree.

These European dallyings with the medicinal use of burning herbs were of little importance compared with what was going on over the unknown curve of the world. The Maya civilisation, which was established in parts of what is now Mexico during the first century B.C., has left behind it a number of magnificent stone temples decorated with clear carvings, among which are several which show priests smoking pipes shaped like a short hunting-horn and made of reeds. The tobacco plant is native to this area, and the smoking of it was, in the beginning, part of the Mayan's religious ceremonies; the smoke was probably puffed out as a form of incense. But the habit spread in the course of the six hundred-odd years of the Mayan civilisation, until it was almost universal among them as a social habit.

When the Mayas, for some still unexplained reason, abandoned their cities and spread to other parts of South America, they took their reed pipes with them. So smoking as a pleasure spread, particularly to the Indians of North America. Here, where palm-leaves, bamboo and suitable reeds were not available, they had to find other ways of holding the burning tobacco, and the first recognisable pipes were made from wood, bone or clay. These have been found in huge quantities in the 'mounds', the characteristic houses-cum-tombs of the early Indians, as far North as what is now the border between the United States and Canada.

But we must return to South America, for it was here that the New World passed the knowledge of tobacco to the Old. In October 1492, Columbus landed in the Bahamas and among other things, received from the astonished natives some dried tobacco leaves. The Spaniards politely waited until they returned to their ships, and then threw them away. After further exploration which reached as far as Cuba, the expedition returned to Spain, bringing with them not a word nor a sample of tobacco. But later explorers who travelled to the Americas, fired by Columbus' tales of riches, did notice the strange habit of the Indians, and brought back descriptions of a kind of Y-shaped pipe; the two upper ends of which were put in the nostrils, and the bottom into a pile of burning tobacco leaves. Other natives in Cuba smoked what were obviously the forerunners of Havana cigars and one traveller even describes a cigar case of woven bast.

By this time (about 1527, thirty-five years after the discovery of the New World) the Spanish settlers had, to a very large extent, fallen under the spell of tobacco themselves, and were heavy smokers. As the ships came and went between Spain and America, the sailors brought back with them first the tales and then the habit. The seed came to Europe in about the middle of the sixteenth century; arriving in Spain, Portugal and France at much the same time. (Portugal had followed hot on the heels of Spain in exploring the new continent, and France had not been slow to realise the possibilities of expansion.) Soon, spreading from the coastal towns, the cultivation of tobacco was common; but it was as a cure-all, not as a recreational pleasure, that it made its mark all over the mainland of Europe. This belief was fostered very largely by the reports of missionaries and other travellers in the wilder parts of South America, who saw the Indians smoking as part of their religious ceremonies; reports like that of the monk Thevet, who, in 1558, sent to Paris a detailed account of the uses of tobacco in Brazil and, after describing the smoking of a sort of cigar, concluded 'this is very good for loosening and carrying off the superfluous humours of the brain'.

It was the sailors who were very largely responsible for the spread of the tobacco habit throughout Europe, but the one figure whose name has gone down through history, firmly attached to tobacco, was a French envoy attached to the Portuguese Court – Jean Nicot. Ironically, it was not for the delights of smoking that he became interested in the plant, but for its wonderful curative powers. Even more ironically, one of the first diseases which tobacco was reputed to cure was cancer. A highly respected Spanish doctor, Nicolo Monardes, published a treatise on the healing powers of the tobacco plant, and this work was soon translated into all the main languages of Europe. Tobacco began to be grown widely throughout Europe, from about 1560 onwards, but always as a medicinal herb; smoking in general was still confined to the seaports. The plant spread to Italy, and from there to Eastern Europe, Turkey and the East.

While the rest of the sixteenth century world was taking to tobacco as the new panacea, England, true to its proud insularity, was proceeding in quite a different direction. From the very first, the English were far more interested in the pleasures they could derive from tobacco, than in its powers to cure all the diseases of man. There has been much argument as to who should have the credit for introducing tobacco into England. Almost certainly it was one of the adventurer sea captains like Drake, Hawkins, or Raleigh, who were warring with the Spaniards off the American coasts from 1558 onwards, to the greater glory of Queen Elizabeth. A strong case can also be made out for Ralph Lane, who returned from governing Virginia in 1586.

The most potent factor in the establishment of smoking in this country as a universal habit was the colony of Virginia, founded by Sir Walter Raleigh in 1584. The colonisation was a complete failure, and within two years all the survivors were back in England, bringing with them, almost to a man, the smoking habit which they had acquired from the Indians. As the colonists returned to their homes all over the country, the practice spread very rapidly, until, by the end of Elizabeth's reign, the whole of England was under the spell. Smoking had become a social necessity, and there were even professors on the subject, who for a fee gave classes in such matters as the art of blowing perfect smoke-rings.

When Elizabeth was succeeded by James I, the carefree atmosphere disappeared overnight, for James was a fanatical hater of tobacco, partly because he thought it was so ruinously expensive that it was having a very considerable effect on the internal economy of the country. To balance this – or at least to ensure that he himself benefitted from it – he raised the duty on tobacco soon after his succession from 2d to the astronomical figure of 6s 10d a pound.

In 1604, James published (anonymously, but this deceived nobody) his celebrated *Counterblaste to Tobacco*, in which he examined at length all the pernicious, debilitating, ruinous effects of what he called 'this precious stinke' – 'precious' because he estimated that some people were expending as much as £400 a year on tobacco, the equivalent of several thousands by to-day's standards. Contemporary records show that in 1589, good tobacco cost 48s a pound. By 1626, this had been reduced to 10s. Another thirty years, however, took only a further 2s off the price of a pound. One observer in 1614 estimated that there were about seven thousand establishments in London selling tobacco.

The result of the King's weighty attack was that the importation of tobacco from abroad (Virginia, now a flourishing colony, had made tobacco cultivation the backbone of its economy) fell slightly, the attacks by English privateers on vessels carrying tobacco from the Spanish-American colonies increased enormously, and the cultivation of the plant in England rose astronomically.

The first mention of snuff-taking in this country is found at about the same time, and was equally condemned by the King's followers. But, in spite of all efforts to stem the tide, including penal import duties, the consumption of tobacco continued to increase steadily year by year. In 1617, a satirical comedy called *The Smoaking Age* was written by Richard Brathwait. The original title page of this play shows a *tabagie*, or smoking shop, in the window of which are a number of items connected with tobacco. These include a wooden blackamoor figure, then as now one of the trade-signs of the tobacco-vendor; clay pipes, all with small bowls and straight stems varying in length from about twelve inches to twenty-four; and another trade sign, a large wooden ball stuck with clay pipes as if it were a giant pomander. In 1620, the Guild of Pipe-Makers was formed in London. James was still trying to perform his hopeless task of prohibiting smoking, and in 1619 he forbade the growing of tobacco in England. Few took any notice. In 1625 James died, to be succeeded by Charles I. Without his father's obsessional hatred of tobacco, he gradually made legal what was already a *fait accompli*, and sensibly turned the trade to his own use by various duties upon home-grown, Virginian and other imported tobacco.

During the first half of the seventeenth century, the habit of smoking, which up to that time had been confined to England, spread to the rest of Europe. As has already been seen, tobacco had been in

use there as a medicinal herb for almost a century, and the new cult
became mixed up with the old. Von Grümmelhausen, a German
observer, put it very well in 1667; commenting acidly on the almost
universal habit of smoking among labourers, he reported that 'some
of them drink their tobacco, some eat it, others sniff it up through
the nostrils – indeed, I am surprized that I have not yet found anyone
plugging his ears with it. But the other methods I have myself seen
practised by persons of all classes, from prince to bishop, from
bishop to barber; and each of them is prepared to explain why he
does it and how it benefits him. One man smokes because it enables
him to see better; another because it disperses water in the brain;
a third to ease his toothache; a fourth to stop the singing in his ears;
a fifth will tell you it makes him sleep; a sixth that it quenches his thirst;
a seventh that it neutralizes the bad effects of too much water-drinking;
an eighth that it expels evil humours; the ninth man smokes to pass the
time; the tenth because he doesn't wish to be unsociable . . . They will
tell you it benefits the peasant who smokes it, the man who prepares it,
the carrier who conveys it, and the merchant or shopkeeper who
deals in it.'

In country after country there was an outcry against the filthy
habit, particularly as the healing properties of tobacco came to be
realised as misrepresentations of the early explorers. The anti-
tobacco factions renewed their attacks when priests began to smoke
and take snuff as a matter of habit during services. The origin of one
habit still with us belongs to this time: Bishop Sarnelli wrote in one
of his letters, 'although it is permissible for a man to use it in case of
necessity, it is certainly not decent to do so in all places and in
general company; consider for instance, that the act of snuff-taking is
apt to result in so violent a sneeze that the hearer is moved to invoke
the help of heaven.' As we still say, 'Bless you.'

In many European countries, smoking was prohibited entirely,
but the results were much the same as they had been in England when
James had tried to suppress it. Even in Turkey, where the penalty was
death, the abolitionists had no better success. By about 1650, when it
had been found that Turkey possessed ideal soil and climate for the
cultivation of the tobacco plant, the Sultan (Mohammed IV, a smoker

himself) repealed the laws, and the growing of tobacco took its place as one of the main enterprises of the country.

By the middle of the seventeenth century, tobacco and the smoking of it was known throughout the world. As soon as each ruler realised the futility of trying to suppress the habit, he also realised that here was an apparently inexhaustible source of revenue. Some kings needed money for wars, some for ambitious building programmes, most for their own private extravagances. One of the first acts of Charles II, after the abdication of Richard Cromwell in 1660, was a statute prohibiting (once more) the growing of tobacco in England, solely because it was depriving him of a large part of his revenue on tobacco which would be imported from Virginia. When this failed, in 1670 he authorised the physical destruction of all plants growing in England and Ireland. This was done by regiments of horsemen galloping over the crops. From that moment tobacco-growing in this country ceased to be an enterprise of any importance.

Virginia, however, prospered enormously as more and more tobacco was exported to England. Not only was the demand doubled almost overnight by the destruction of the home plantations, but the new habit of snuff-taking was becoming wide-spread among the upper classes, further increasing consumption from the American colonies. One strange byway of the story of tobacco was its use by some ladies of this time as a dentifrice and a sweetener of the breath. One does not imagine however that this had a significant effect upon the figures of tobacco consumption in general.

Just as pipe-smoking had spread throughout the European and Eastern world from England, so it was France that introduced this next major revolution in the use of tobacco. Snuff (which in its basic form is no more than finely-ground tobacco leaves) had been seen in use by Columbus among the American Indians, but it had not commended itself to European noses as a general habit. The change from smoking to snuff-taking among the French aristocracy was caused less by the continuing outcry of clergy and doctors, as by the incompatibility of gracious living, on the scale practised by the Court of Louis XIII, with permanent clouds of acrid smoke. Snuff, with its rapidly-developed little rituals and mannerisms, and the opportunity it gave for beautiful miniature containers, began to oust the pipe from about 1640.

In England, the new French fashion of snuffing very rapidly conquered the old-established pipe; all things French, at the height of Louis XIV's magnificence, were the rage. The process was certainly hastened by the flood of Huguenot craftsmen who fled from the persecutions resulting from the revocation of the Edict of Nantes in 1685. How successfully snuff ousted the pipe from fashionable circles is shown in Macaulay's description (in his *History of England from the accession of James II*) of the coffee-houses at this time – 'The atmosphere was like that of a perfumer's shop. Tobacco in any other form than that of richly scented snuff was held in abomination. If any clown, ignorant of the usages of the house, called for a pipe, the sneers of the whole assembly and the short answers of the waiters soon convinced him that he had better go somewhere else. Nor, indeed, would he have had far to go. For, in general, the coffee rooms reeked with tobacco like a guard room, and strangers sometimes expressed their surprise that so many people should leave their own firesides to sit in the midst of eternal fog and stench.'

Not only in England, but all over the world, the taxation of tobacco in all its forms had become an established part of the financial structure. A common way for the tax to be levied was the granting of a monopoly, in return for a substantial consideration, to some major figure of the exclusive right to grow and sell tobacco.

The Plague, which ravaged the whole of Europe during the second half of the seventeenth century, and which came to London in 1665, was a major factor in the spread of the habit among all classes and both sexes of society. Even in England, which had not taken to the notion that tobacco was a cure-all as had most of the rest of the world, the idea that tobacco-smoking might be at least disinfectant was seized upon when all other remedies failed. Boys at Eton were required by magisterial command to smoke a pipe every morning; and Pepys recorded in his diary how he suddenly felt ill at the sight of the stark red crosses painted on the doors of plague-ridden houses, and bought a roll of tobacco to smoke and chew. The air of London was perpetually full of the haze from tobacco pipes during that terrible year – smoke which was replaced by the far greater volumes which rolled up from the Great Fire in 1666. Strangely enough, it was not a burning pipe which caused the Great Fire, but a spontaneous blaze in a tallow-chandler's shop.

The arrival of snuff in England was occasioned by the return of Charles II, who had spent much of his exile in France, and whose courtiers were very largely French in their habits. For the whole period of the Stuart monarchy and until the End of the Georgian Era, snuff was the only fashionable way of using tobacco, although it should be made clear that the habits of the fashionable minority on the one hand, and the mass of English peasantry on the other, were two vastly different things. While tobacco smoking was 'out' in Court Circles, probably more tobacco was smoked per head of the population than at any time in our history until the introduction of the cigarette.

It was enjoyed impartially by both sexes, and many of the beautiful and ornate snuff-boxes which have come down to us from this period were ladies' possessions. Some women of character, in spite of the prevailing fashion, continued to smoke their pipes. One, a certain Madame Lencorande, wrote a little book in 1715 in defence of the habit, entitled *A Sound and Pleasant Proof that a Respectable Woman may sometimes enter a Coffee-house without Damage to her Good Name, and moreover she may, and should, treat herself to a Pipe of Tobacco. Further it is also explained why Women go first, and why Men wear Beards. All most briefly and pleasantly proved, and maintained by Incontestable Reasons.* A German author some few years later produced a satire called *Lust of the Longing Nose,* in which he said 'The world has taken up a ridiculous fashion – the excessive use of snuff. All nations are snuffing. All classes snuff, from the highest to the lowest. I have sometimes wondered to see how lords and lackeys, High Society and the mob, woodchoppers and handymen, broom-squires and beadles, take out their snuff-boxes with an air, and dip into them. Both sexes snuff, for the fashion has spread to the women; the ladies began it, and are now imitated by the washerwoman. People snuff so often that their noses are more like a dust-heap than a nose.'

As the years of the eighteenth century went by, snuff-taking became such a universal habit that it seemed as if smoking were dying out completely. In 1773, Dr Johnson said with an air of righteousness 'Smoking has gone out. To be sure, it is a shocking thing, blowing smoke out of our mouths into other people's mouths, eyes and noses, and having the same thing done to us'. But just when it really did seem that smoking would never reappear (even the undergraduates at Oxford and Cambridge had practically given it up for snuffing), the cigar made its appearance.

Cigars of a kind were enjoyed by the Indians that Columbus met at the end of the fifteenth century. These were usually rolled-up palm-leaves filled with tobacco. They were developed, particularly in the Spanish American colonies, into rolls of tobacco-leaf, often with a straw set in the middle to help the cigars to draw. The first real contact that the English made with Spain and Spanish habits came in the course of the Peninsular war at the beginning of the nineteenth century. The British soldiers (and the French and Germans too) took immediately to the new habit and, when the Napoleonic wars at last ended at Waterloo in 1815, they brought their taste for 'segars' home with them.

Almost as rapidly as snuff-taking had ousted the pipe from fashionable circles, the cigar overcame the snuff-box. As a sign of the times, a special smoking room was set aside in the Houses of Parliament within fifteen years of the end of the war. But the way of smokers was not strewn with roses, particularly with two such violently anti-smoking figures as Queen Victoria and the Duke of Wellington in the forefront of the nation's activities. It is recorded that guests at Windsor were compelled to blow their smoke up the chimneys in case the Queen should catch the scent of tobacco in the air.

Wellington's order to the army in 1845 was in its language very similar to the outburst of over two hundred years before:

'The Commander-in-Chief has been informed that the practice of smoking, by the use of pipes, cigars, or cheroots, has become prevalent among the officers of the Army, which is not only in itself a species of intoxication occasioned by the fumes of tobacco, but, undoubtedly, occasions drinking and tippling by those who acquire the habit; and he intreats the Officers commanding Regiments to prevent smoking in the Mess Rooms of their several Regiments, and in the adjoining apartments, and to discourage the practice among the Officers of Junior Rank in their Regiments.'

It was the revolutions that broke out all over Europe in 1848 that finally spelt emancipation to European smokers, who in some cities and principalities had still been suppressed and threatened with severe penalties for smoking in public.

Although the cigar, in its turn, declined in popularity in England with the introduction of the cigarette, most Continental countries remain firmly attached to it to this day. Indeed, only the French-speaking countries smoke cigarettes in preference to cigars, and their brand of tobacco has its own peculiar qualities.

The cigarette first appeared in South America, rough tobacco leaves being rolled inside a thin paper tube. France was the first European country to use them, in about 1844, but it was another war which spread the new habit to the rest of Europe. The meeting together of the English, Turks and French against the Russians in the Crimea, and the subsequent dispersal of the soldiers to their homes, accomplished for the cigarette exactly what the Peninsular war of half a century earlier had done for the cigar.

The early cigarettes were villainous affairs on account of the poor quality of the tobacco used in them (one rolled one's own in those days) and met with a very considerable outcry on their first appearance in England. The first manufactured cigarettes appeared in Austria in 1865. It was a long (about nine inches) paper tube packed with tobacco of reasonably good quality; there was a mouthpiece at each end, and the smoker broke the cigarette in half before using it. It was a few years before the invention, by way of London, reached America where it became an immediate success.

So the wheel came a full circle, from South America where pipe smoking began, through Europe and back to North America a hundred years ago, in the form of the cigarette. What the next development in the habit will be, and whether medical opinion will banish smoking altogether, only time will tell. In the succeeding chapters, we shall be looking in some detail at the tools of the smoker.

2. Pipes

If you collected a hundred visitors from Venus, put them down in different parts of the world, and told them each to make something out of the materials available, from which they could breathe in tobacco smoke, you would certainly get at least ninety different ideas – always assuming that the Venusians have not already learned to smoke. Even without extra-terrestrial help, different peoples have produced pipes so utterly unlike any others that it is often difficult to see that they were all intended for the same purpose. At the end of this chapter we will mention some of the more exotic kinds of pipes from all over the world which a collector might come across.

So far as English smoking is concerned, however, there is only one kind of pipe of any historical importance – the clay.

Clay Pipes

It is unfortunately true that a collector has as much chance of stumbling across a Stradivarius as he has of finding a late sixteenth or early seventeenth century clay pipe in perfect condition. They were horribly fragile, in spite of the protective cases sometimes made for them. More significantly, they were from the start intended to be completely expendible.

An eighteenth century gentleman, for example, bought his pipes by the gross, or the dozen gross, and might easily get through half a dozen clays in a day if he were a busy man, changing clothes and moving from place to place. It is hardly surprising that early clays are considerable rarities.

The reader might think that old clay pipes would make a

particularly dull subject for a collection. In fact, you can get as much information from the shape of a clay pipe as you can from the shape of a chair – more, very often, for not a few of the pipe-makers were proud enough of their pipes to sign them.

The earliest clay pipes are distinguished mainly by their tiny bowls. Tobacco, until the colony of Virginia got into its stride by about 1625, was ruinously expensive – the equivalent today of several pounds an ounce, and that at a time before governments were adding twice the original cost in taxation. In spite of the cost the English, who led the world in this form of tobacco consumption, were seldom without a clay pipe in their mouths. As early as 1598, a German traveller marvelled at us and our clay pipes, puffing out smoke through our nostrils 'like funnels, along with it plenty of phlegm and defluxtion from the head' as he said.

These first clays were less than an inch in height, and are sometimes known as 'fairy pipes' (for obvious reasons) or 'Roman Pipes', from the belief that anything dug out of the ground must be Roman. The very small size of the bowl was only partly the result of the high cost of tobacco on its first introduction. More significant was the tiny bowl of the pipes smoked by the North American Indians at this time, for reasons of ceremony rather than economy. The early Virginian settlers copied these exactly, and returned to England with pipes holding no more than a pinch of tobacco – pipes which the English pipe-makers used as a pattern.

The most characteristic shape of these earliest clays was a short, tilted-forward barrel, resting on a flat heel. The stems as a rule were about twelve inches long, though both shorter and longer ones were made. Decoration of any kind was rare; occasionally the mouth of the bowl was edged with an engraved line of milling. The maker's mark, in the form of initials or a symbol, was on some occasions stamped on the heel. Examples can be seen in one of the few collections of sixteenth century clays in the country, at the Guildhall Museum in London.

This attractive, barrel-shaped bowl lasted, in modified forms, throughout the long life of the clay pipe. Another sixteenth century form was unique to this period. Here, the bowl was no more than a

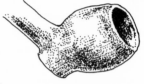

Clay pipe bowls:
the approximate dates are (top) 1600 (centre) 1630 and (bottom) 1700

thickening of the already very substantial stem, turned very slightly upwards to stop the tobacco falling out, and sometimes finished with a rim. The capacity of such a bowl was about the same as an acorn cup, and the 'heel' was merely a flattened area where the stem joined the bowl. Even such crude affairs as these were sometimes marked with their makers' name.

The main development in clay pipes, between the end of the sixteenth and the middle of the seventeenth century, was in the size of the bowl. Tobacco by this time had become very considerably cheaper – about a fifth of the price it had been in 1600 – and clay pipe bowls reflected the trend. They still retained, as they did for at least a century to come, the forward lean of the bulbous bowl. Typical of many pipes of the period were those made by the Hunt family of Bristol. The bowl was comparatively long and narrow, with a marked double curve, and a prominent flat heel on which the maker's mark was stamped. In the case of the Hunts, there were at least four members of the family who made clay pipes and each signed his (or her) own models – John, Jeffrey, Thomas and Flower, sometimes in full, sometimes as initials. Other known pipe-makers of the period were Thomas Smith, Humphrey Partridge, Richard Nummery, Philip Edwards and S. Wheticker.

Deposits of excellent pipe clay were found at Broseley in Staffordshire, and many pipe works were established nearby early in the seventeenth century. The name Broseley soon became synonymous with first-class clay pipes, a label which remained for more than three hundred years until clay pipes were virtually no more. Hull and Nottingham also became well-known centres.

A particularly celebrated pipe maker at this time was Gauntlett of Winchester, whose attractively-shaped bowls were marked at the bottom, on the flat heel, with his mark of a glove. His pipes were sufficiently in demand for the mark to have been imitated, not only in England but in Holland too.

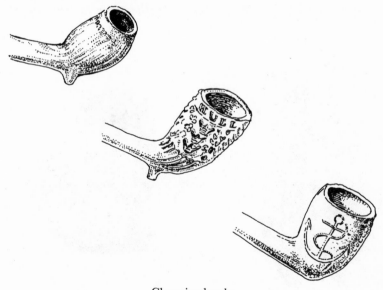

Clay pipe bowls:
the approximate dates are (top) 1720 (centre) 1800 and (bottom) 1870

Although in England, average quality pipes now sold at about half a crown a gross, clay pipes were objects of some value in the American colonies. It is recorded that in 1677 one hundred and twenty clay pipes and one hundred jews' harps were exchanged with Indians for a strip of land in New Jersey.

By about 1690, some makers were producing pipes with a less pronounced forward lean, and without the double curve (known as an Ogee curve). Also, at about this time, the flat heel began to be replaced by a spur, a change which became standard in the eighteenth century. The loss of the flat heel meant that the maker's mark was now stamped either on the bowl or on the stem.

The main contribution of the eighteenth century to the development of the clay pipe was in decoration and the length of the stem. Up to this stage, pipe bowls had been decorated very sparsely, if at all, and stems were usually straight and not more than a foot long. It must be remembered that clay was still, for practical purposes, the only material from which pipes were made. It was to be expected

Decorative clay pipe bowls

that the great artistic upheaval of the eighteenth century would also
have its effect upon even such simple affairs as clay pipes, when they
were smoked by rich and poor alike. The eighteenth century was the
time when snuff practically ousted tobacco smoking as the fashionable
form of taking tobacco, and the impression is sometimes given that
smoking died out altogether. Nothing could be further from the
truth. The great majority of countrymen, and the labourers in towns,
were inseparable from their pipes and took not the slightest notice
of fashion. Many rich men too cared little for fashionable whims and
were too fond of smoking to give it up.

But the clay pipe makers at least noticed the revolution in
artistic taste, and eighteenth century pipes have bowls of simpler
shape, but decorated to a greater or lesser degree, usually with
mouldings in the clay. The stems are, in general, longer and curved
downwards, though not to the extent, either in length or curvature,
of the 'Churchwarden' pipe, an early nineteenth century invention –
also known as a 'yard of clay'.

Although we are mainly concerned with English clay pipes, mention
must be made of Dutch clays for comparison, because they were turned
out in enormous numbers over much the same period. As it happens,
nearly all the clay pipes made in Holland were produced from English
clay exported there. This infuriated the Guild of Tobacco-Pipe Makers
(founded in 1619), particularly as a large proportion of the finished
Dutch clays were re-exported back to England and sold here in direct
competition with their own members' products. They petitioned
Parliament in 1663 to stop the export of pipe clay, and this was
granted. It is almost certain that the first Dutch clay pipe makers
learned their trade in England and copied English designs. The early
(second half of the seventeenth century) pipes from Holland tend to
have longer stems than their English counterparts, to be decorated
more often with incised lines or stylised patterns, and in some cases
to have stems which curve upwards, unlike the straight or slightly
downward-curving stems of English clays. The stem was often tipped
with red wax, a fashion copied by England. The development of the
heel into a spur followed a similar time-scale in Holland and in
England, and was caused by the lengthening of the stem. A short,

straight-stemmed pipe would rest upright on a table on its heel, but the longer, curved-stem pipe required a stand when not in use, and a projection – the spur – to keep the hot bowl away from polished furniture when in action.

As is so often true in the field of collecting, the clay pipe which has attracted the most popular attention is not truly representative. The 'Churchwarden' pipe with its long curved stem was never a popular model among true smokers of the clay pipe, and indeed was introduced as a novelty. They were modelled on a form of clay pipe which had a vogue round about 1700, with a rather longer stem than the usual twelve inches, tipped with glaze to form a mouth-piece, and known as an 'Alderman'.

The main vogue of the Churchwarden was in the middle of the nineteenth century, when pipe smokers who normally smoked the short 'cutty' during the day would gather at the inn in the evening to smoke in a more leisured way. At this time, it was perfectly acceptable for the upper classes to smoke short clay pipes; the 'snob value' came from buying the clay from a fashionable maker such as Milo in London or Fiolet at St Omer. As in the case of the later *Meerschaum*, there was considerable rivalry among gentlemen in the art of colouring a clay pipe by smoking it under careful control; Fiolet pipes were particularly good in this respect. The nineteenth and early twentieth centuries saw pipes made in which the bowls were fairly crudely modelled into heads of well-known contemporary figures such as Gladstone and Admiral Jellicoe.

Although clay was practically without a rival for pipe-smoking for 250 years, the sheer exclusiveness of tobacco in the very earliest years of its introduction to this country caused the pioneer smokers – rich men by the evidence that they could afford to smoke at all – to have costly pipes made for their special use. Some had silver pipes made in the form of imitation clays – a strange example of the usual copying process in reverse. There was also a brief vogue for iron pipes in the eighteenth century, but they never became at all popular with true addicts.

At the other end of the scale, a walnut shell pierced for a straw stem made an adequate pipe according to the seventeenth century diarist John Aubrey, until the manufacturers of clays could supply the evergrowing demand at prices which the poor could pay.

Mention should be made of the celebrated French clay pipes of the period between the end of the eighteenth century and about 1870. Until the Napoleonic period, French clays had followed the pattern of English products, both in shape and simplicity, but in about 1790 several factories began to make well-modelled pipes in the form of heads. The subjects were usually contemporary or historical figures, and some of the earliest were modelled on the leaders of the Revolution – Robespierre, Mirabeau, Marat, Napoleon himself. Foreign celebrities were also used as models, among them Queen Victoria.

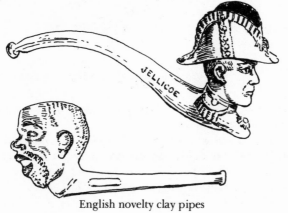

English novelty clay pipes

Apart from these seriously intended designs, a large number of complete fantasies were produced to appeal to simpler and earthier humours – grotesque heads and skulls, animals and so on. Certainly the most amusing is a caricature of the Duke of Wellington (already mentioned as a violent non-smoker, and of course a heartily-loathed figure to every Frenchman) with, immediately behind, a French soldier thumbing his nose.

The most famous factories were those of Fiolet at St Omer and Gambier of Paris. The firm at St Omer (one of several there) introduced enamel colours on to their products, with great success. Most

French clay of about 1810

French clays of this type were made as bowls only, allowing for a stem of some other material to be inserted.

The only serious European rivals to clay, as a material for pipe-making during the eighteenth century, were porcelain and meers-chaum both of which are dealt with more fully in succeeding pages. It was once again the artistic revolution of this period which led to a demand for more elegant forms of pipe, a demand which was adequately filled by these two materials.

Meerschaum Pipes

The merits of Meerschaum pipes, like the briars which followed them, were discovered largely by accident, if the generally accepted stories of the origin of both are to be believed. Meerschaum in German means sea-foam, and it is a word which the English, unlike the French, have never bothered to translate (the French transliterated it to *écume-de-mer*). In its natural state, this form of magnesium silicate looks not unlike petrified foam, and it is sometimes still washed up on the shores of the Black Sea.

It was in Central Europe that meerschaum was first used for making pipe bowls. According to legend it was a Budapest shoemaker who found the secret of 'colouring' the material by the use of wax. This took place in about 1750, so meerschaum must have been used for pipes before this. It has the essential merits of any material which is to be used for holding burning tobacco – a degree of porosity, insulating properties, the ability to produce a 'cool' smoke, even and slow carbonisation. It is also easily carved. But nobody should imagine that a coat of cobbler's wax will produce the glorious, even colour of a fine meerschaum which was the pride of every Victorian smoker.

Wax was certainly an essential ingredient, but it was the actual smoking of the pipe which wrought the change (meerschaum in its natural state is almost pure white). There is a well-known story of the owner of a newly-bought meerschaum pipe, which illustrates both the process and the mystique of colouring. It was first told by Fairholt in his *Tobacco* published in 1859. There was a smoker 'who, determined to have a perfect meerschaum – it being understood that perfection cannot be attained if the pipe once lighted be allowed to cool – made arrangements that it should pass from mouth to mouth of a regiment of soldiers, the owner of the pipe paying the bill. After seven months a perfect pipe was handed to the owner with a tobacco bill for more

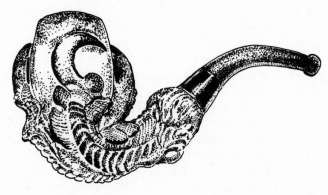

Late nineteenth century Meerschaum pipe

than one hundred pounds'. Whether this particular tale is true or not, enormous trouble was taken by dedicated smokers to ensure that their meerschaum was properly and evenly coloured. Colours can range from a pale amber to a brown so dark as to be almost black, and some addicts preferred that their pipes should be graded in colour throughout this range.

The ease with which meerschaum can be carved was fully exploited; some of the finer examples can be compared with Japanese netsuke, those intricately-fashioned ivory toggles beloved of oriental collectors, in their skilful elaboration. Subjects vary enormously. Probably the most common are human heads, male and female. Complete human figures, lying or sitting and cleverly incorporated into the angle where the bowl joins the stem, are also still to be found in some numbers. Animals, children, battle and hunting scenes, ships, mythological scenes – all these are known; the variety is enormous. Almost without exception, meerschaum pipes were made to be fitted with a mouth-piece of another material; amber was a favourite, for the sake of the harmony of its natural colour with the painstakingly coloured meerschaum.

Dating of meerschaum pipes is difficult and not particularly rewarding. The earliest pipes to reach this country were imported in the late seventeen fifties, and their popularity lasted almost exactly a hundred years, until they began to be superseded by the briar in about 1860 (although as always happens, some devotees refused to fall in with the new fashion; meerschaum pipes were made in some quantity in this country well into the present century and are still produced today). The earliest pipes were sparsely decorated and had comparatively large bowls into which a long wooden or ivory tube was inserted as a stem and mouthpiece. The more elaborate carvings were not seen in quantity until about 1830.

One elaborate fake in meerschaum pipes is made up of a heavy bowl, sparingly and somewhat crudely carved, and fitted with a mouthpiece decorated with mother-of-pearl. Pipes of this kind were produced in quantity in about 1890, and were made from meerschaum parings moulded and pressed together. Often a spurious date, up to one hundred years earlier, is incorporated in the carving.

A more certain method of dating is by means of the hall-mark on the silver band which often covers the join between the short stem of the meerschaum bowl and the mouthpiece.

Meerschaum was also used extensively as holders for cigars and cigarettes, both of which were introduced to this country during the nineteenth century. More will be said of these holders in the appropriate chapters.

Porcelain Pipes

Porcelain pipes have never been popular in England, happily married as it was to its old clay. 'The execrable china pipe is the mystery of the German' one writer said in 1876. 'It has no absorption. It is a mere tobacco-still, condensing the fetid juices in its reservoir which must be frequently emptied and cleaned, or it is converted into a hubble-bubble of disgusting poison'. The reference to the lack of absorbtion is of some importance, for it is this factor which gives the German porcelain pipe its characteristic shape.

Unglazed clay allows most of the liquids which gather in the bowl of the pipe to evaporate to the outside air through the pores in the material. Glazed porcelain seals these liquids in however, and a means had to be found of separating them from the burning tobacco.

The final answer was found towards the end of the eighteenth century, but porcelain pipes were being made about thirty years before that. Until the seventeen sixties, clay pipes were smoked in Germany, as they were throughout the smoking world. It is not clear why Germany, and to a lesser extent its neighbours, should have taken to the new medium, but it was appropriate for the home of European porcelain-making.

Both the Meissen and the Nymphenburg factories produced porcelain pipe heads in considerable quantity from 1765 onwards, and other establishments were not slow to follow. The earliest productions differ from all later ones by being in the form of modelled (and usually enamelled) heads and figures, human and animal. Modelling was later reduced to relief work on the generally cylindrical shape

Austrian
porcelain
pipes

of the bowl; and by the beginning of the nineteenth century, the familiar painted bowl was almost universal. Some moulded pipes were produced again much later.

The tall, narrow, cylindrical bowl of the most common type of nineteenth century porcelain pipe ends in a short stem which is bent only very slightly from the axis of the bowl, and finished with a knob on the underside. The short stem fits not into a longer stem ending in a mouthpiece, but into a Y-shaped porcelain reservoir which collects the juices and which can be emptied out at frequent intervals. Into the other arm of the Y fits the long stem and mouthpiece, which may be made of almost any suitable material, such as wood, horn, ivory, or bone. The pipe is normally smoked at waist level, the stem rising from the reservoir almost vertically.

The subjects of the painting on porcelain pipe bowls vary as much as they do on snuff-box lids, although in both cases there is perhaps a majority of pretty girls. The early examples (up to about 1850) are hand-painted, but thereafter transfer-printing was the rule. Only in rare cases was the Y-shaped porcelain reservoir decorated in one with the bowl. Porcelain pipes are still made today in Austria and Bavaria; in general, they are crude and garish; the collector should have no difficulty in separating the eighteenth and nineteenth century sheep from the twentieth century goats.

Returning to England, some extremely interesting pipes were made in *pottery* during the eighteenth century. Most of these were certainly intended for show rather than use. Among them are the amusing 'puzzle' pipes made by Pratt towards the end of the century. These are not really puzzles at all, but merely an enormously long narrow tube formed into a bowl at one end and a mouthpiece at the other, and then coiled and knotted while the clay was still plastic to make an awkwardly-shaped but smokeable pipe through which the smoke would eventually reach the smoker. There were many patterns of this particular joke – a popular one was a snake, brightly decorated and with the pipe bowl disappearing down its throat. Other delicately made and attractive coloured 'show' pipes were made in Staffordshire during the century, by not only the famous potters – Astbury, Whieldon, Pratt – but a host of others also. One of the best-known designs was the 'heart-in-hand' pipe, in which the clay pipe, decorated with coloured glazes and modelled into a female head, was held by the fingers of a modelled hand in the palm of which is a red heart.

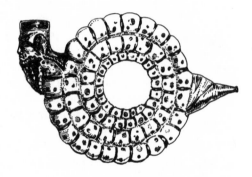

Pottery pipes

Glass Pipes

Equally attractive as the pottery pipes, but even less suitable for practical smoking, were the glass pipes made at the Bristol factory and other glass-making establishments during the eighteenth and early nineteenth centuries. These were exercises in the art of glass-making rather than commercial pieces.

Glass Pipe

Wooden Pipes

Wooden pipes were smoked by a few determinedly eccentric English smokers but never became popular because of their essential disadvantage of burning themselves away not much less slowly than the tobacco they contained. This drawback was removed however with the discovery of the briar.

The modern briar, which has completely ousted all other conventional forms of pipe in Europe and America, has a comparatively long history. Its discovery, according to the accepted story, was quite accidental. A French pipe-maker, visiting Corsica in 1825 to pay his respects to Napoleon's birthplace, lost or broke his meerschaum and asked a local man to carve him a temporary replacement. The Corsican used a piece of root from the *bruyère,* the heath tree. The finished pipe was a revelation, and the pipe-maker took some pieces of the root back to France with him, and so founded the industry. The virtues of the briar as a material for pipe bowls are its hardness and fine grain, its durability (clay and meerschaum were both very fragile), lightness, poor conduction of heat, and its resistance to fire. Incidentally, France exports most of its production of briar pipes to England, the first of which came in about 1859. The name briar has nothing to do with the briar rose, but is merely a corruption of the French.

There are many other types of pipe which the collector will meet in this country. Most of them have been brought from abroad by travellers as decorative curiosities, for smoking habits change extremely slowly, not least in this country.

Tube Pipes

The most basic form of pipe is the plain tube, fashioned from whatever suitable material is readily to hand – bamboo, or cane, or a twig or bone, decorated or undecorated according to the fancy of the maker. Pipes of this kind are still made by primitive peoples, particularly in South-East Asia and South America, and among Australian bushmen. Tube-pipes in pottery are also characteristic of many ancient races, more especially in South America.

More complex pipes on the tube pattern are still smoked today in Afghanistan and Japan.

Mound Pipes

The Red Indians of North America left behind, in their burial mounds as prized possessions, pipes of a characteristic shape which seem to be unique to this part of the world. The stem of the pipe is flat and downward – curving, and the bowl is set in the middle of the stem instead of at one end of it. Almost without exception, these 'mound pipes' as they have come to be known, are carved from extremely hard stone – granite or porphyry are the most common. Without departing from the basic shape of the central bowl on a downward-curving flat stem, the makers produced some most attractive designs. Favourite subjects were animals, fish and birds, all carved with great realism on top of the stem, to form the bowl.

It is noticeable that these animal figures were carved to face the smoker, rather than away from him as one would perhaps have expected. Human heads of typical North American Indian cast are also known. Just how old the mound pipes are is not clear, although modern techniques of dating by radioactivity will no doubt be used. But it is certain that the earliest of them were being smoked long before tobacco came to the Old World.

While we are dealing with the North American Indians, mention should be made of what is probably the best-known kind of pipe in the world –

The Pipe of Peace

Before the Indians lost their lands and their independence and became no more than tourist attractions, the calumet was one of the most important possessions of each tribe. Its short, conical bowl was made from a special red clay reserved for this one purpose and quarried in one sacred place by all tribes. The stem was four or five feet long, and decorated in a style which was individual to each tribe. Eagle feathers formed a large part of the decorative scheme. The only time the calumet was ever used was at the agreeing of a peace treaty.

The War Pipe was regarded with less reverence. It was a tomahawk, the handle hollowed out to form the stem, and a pipe bowl fixed opposite the blade.

It is interesting that it was from Indians of the south-east corner of the area which is now the United States of America that the habit of smoking was first learned by Europeans; and that pipes from the burial mounds of Indians in this area are of the familiar 'bent-up-end' shape. These early travellers obviously copied what they saw when they returned to Europe. One could speculate on what our smoking habits might now have been if we had learned to smoke from the 'earth-smokers' of parts of Africa and India, who construct a little clay mound on the bare earth, make a hole in the top for the tobacco and another at the side as a mouthpiece. Smoking such a pipe requires the smoker to lie flat on his face.

Indians of the north-western area of America produced very

elaborately-carved pipes in slate, the designs again being taken largely from natural sources.

Eskimo Pipes

Among Eskimos, a typical pipe of the western area (nearest the influence of Asiatic smoking) is made up from a bowl, carved in stone, with a very small aperture for the tobacco and a wide rim round the top. This bowl is lashed with rawhide strips to an upward-curving stem of wood. Eskimo pipes of ivory (from walrus-tusks), beautifully decorated with carved pictorial scenes, are much sought-after.

Japanese and Chinese Pipes

Typical Japanese pipes are long and straight-stemmed, with a tiny bowl, usually of metal cast in the shape of an acorn. Chinese pipes are larger but of the same general pattern. Both Chinese and Japanese pipes are often decorated with enormous care, and some were turned into works of great beauty in materials such as jade, ivory, or lacquer.

Water Pipes

One common method of smoking in the East which differs radically from that practised in Europe makes use of a container of water between the bowl and the mouthpiece. This allows the smoke to be cleaned and cooled before it reaches the smoker. The commonest way to achieve this was to mount the bowl on a short stem which was then pushed into a larger tube of some suitable material, closed at one end and filled with water. The mouthpiece was the other end of the tube and the pipe was held at such an angle that smoke from the tobacco passed down the stem into the water in the large tube, bubbled through it and so reached the smoker. This is the principle of the *dakka* (or hemp) pipe common in much of Africa.

The Indian *Nargileh* is a similar adaptation, in which (originally) the water vessel was a coconut shell, the pipe bowl stuck in the top on a short stem and the mouthpiece a tube projecting from the side. The coconut shell was soon replaced by more elaborate and beautiful containers, and the fixed mouth-piece became a tube early in the eighteenth century. The nargileh and the similar *hookah* were both intended for leisurely smoking, often on a communal basis.

When the Chinese adapted the water pipe, however, they produced an individual and typical smoking apparatus. This is made entirely of metal and has a long vertical stem, curving only at the mouthpiece, joined to a small water chamber, on top of which is a tube containing the tiny tobacco bowl.

3. Pipe Accessories

Pipe Burners

The modern briar pipe with its short, detachable stem is easily enough cleaned with one of those flexible pipe-cleaners that have almost as ready a sale for fashioning into dogs and donkeys and other mantle-piece animals. The problem, at first sight, was more difficult to solve in the days when the pipes were long-stemmed, fragile clays. The answer, however, was very simple. It was soon found that if a foul clay pipe was put bodily into the kitchen fire, it emerged purged of all the

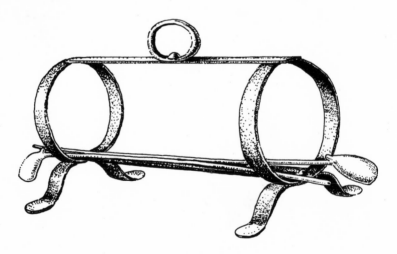

Pipe burning rack

sediment in the bowl and stem, and needed only a wash to be almost
as good as new. Many of the more comfortable households did not
bother to clean their pipes at all, but simply threw them away when
they became foul, for pipes were cheap enough in the seventeenth and
eighteenth centuries to buy by the gross.

The impecunious countryman had the local blacksmith make him
an iron pipe kiln.

Pipe-burning Rack, or Pipe Kiln

In its simplest form the pipe kiln consisted of two iron rings about
four inches across, joined by a strip top and bottom which held the
rings a foot or so apart. The rack was provided with feet so that it could

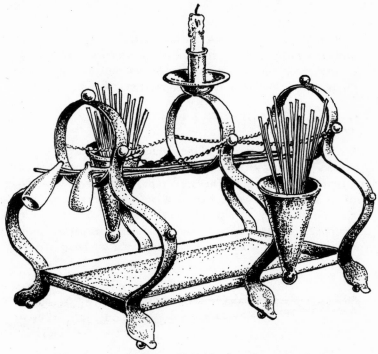

Combination pipe burner, spill-holder, candlestand and ashtray

be stood in the hearth. In use, several clay pipes were put into the rack with the stems through the two rings. It was then lowered into the flames of the kitchen fire by means of a ring attached to the upper strip, or (more commonly) put into a hot oven. Country bakers would often make it one of their sidelines to collect and bake clay pipes in their bread ovens.

There were many local variations of the basic shape (known as a 'two-ring' burner). 'Three-ring' burners, which gave extra support in the middle to the pipe stem, were as common, and 'two-and-a-half ring' models were also made. A more elaborate model is in the Victoria and Albert Museum. This is a sort of smoker's companion, and was obviously not intended to put into the fire; the central ring is crowned by a candle-holder, and two spill-holders are attached to the elaborate legs. Fixed to the feet and held an inch or so off the ground is a tray on which ash and spent spills could be put.

When they were not in use for their main purpose, pipe burners stood in the hearth to hold pipes and to warm them ready for smoking. Very many iron burners were made in Sussex, the centre of the English iron industry in the seventeenth and early eighteenth centuries.

Tobacco Tongs

There are two distinct types of the eighteenth and nineteenth century smokers' tools known variously as tobacco tongs, pipe tongs, ember tongs and smokers' tongs. The larger type, normally made of wrought iron or steel, were used to take up a glowing ember from the fire to light a pipe. They appeared towards the end of the seventeenth century. Not a few are dated, and some bear their owner's initials; others were lovingly decorated with engraving and chamfered edges.

Steel smokers' tongs

Although details of design differ considerably between examples, a common feature is the steel leaf-spring between the handles. The tongs were used in one hand, for obvious reasons, and the spring kept the jaws closed against the ember when it had been taken from the fire. The jaws themselves were usually broadened into gripping surfaces, and were often amusingly decorated – a hand or a shell was a favourite symbol. The jaws of one particularly fine example in the Guildhall Museum are formed into a pair of hearts. It was quite common for the ends of the handles (or, more usually, one of them) to be fashioned into tobacco stoppers. The eighteenth century tongs in the Guildhall Museum already mentioned go one stage further, for both handles end in stoppers, one of which unscrews and turns round to become a pricker.

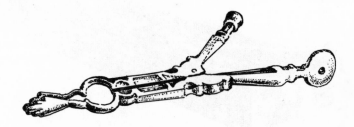

Brass tinder tongs

The other, and smaller, type of tobacco tongs were more usually made in brass, and were designed to pick up a piece of smouldering tinder from the tinder box; they were often part of the equipment of the tinderbox itself. These also vary widely in shape, but are generally in the form of miniature fire-side tongs with a single handle and hinged arms. The handle is often formed into a tobacco stopper as in the case of the larger ember tongs. One form is made in springy steel like a pair of tweezers.

An unusual type of ember tong was fitted with a whistle in one of the handles. These were used in inns, the whistle being used to call the pot-boy.

Pipe Racks

Several quite different types of box or holder to support pipes when not in use are to be found. The simplest is a horizontal wooden strip pierced with holes. The strip was fixed to the wall and the stems of the pipes passed through the holes so that the bowls rested on the strip. This is probably the earliest pipe rack, and it was made both for domestic use and for inns, where clay pipes were available for customers to use. A development of this simple wooden rack allowed a number of long-stemmed clay pipes to rest horizontally in slots cut in two wooden uprights.

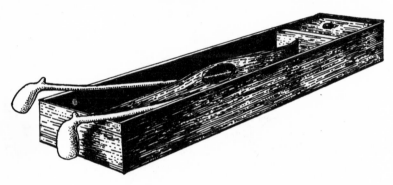

Wooden clay pipe case

A common eighteenth century alternative to the wall rack for these long-stemmed clays was an open box, rather like a large cutlery tray, but with the central division curved to allow the stems of the pipes to fit inside. A lidded compartment was often provided at one end of the box to contain flint and steel.

Another more elegant type of pipe rack also provided a means of lighting the pipe. This was in the form of a long candlestick on a large circular base; a few inches below the candle was a wooden disc about eight inches across, pierced with holes for the pipe stem. The bowls rested in depressions cut into the base. Some examples of the early nineteenth century are also provided with spill-containers.

Clay pipe stand

Clay Pipe-making Tools

The making of clay pipes in this country can be traced back at least to 1563, when a Statute enacted that nobody could make clay tobacco pipes until they had served a five-year apprenticeship. In 1601 a monopoly was granted to the Tobacco-Pipe Makers' Company (who were granted a charter in 1619), a monopoly which lasted for over two hundred years until the makers of the new briar pipes began to complain.

Clay pipes required a good deal of handwork, but little space to make them in. The workshops and the kilns were small, and the makers highly-skilled. A pipe would start off as a lump of raw clay, pounded and kneaded to make it workable and free from lumps and impurities. This was then rolled by hand into a 'sausage' of the right length, rather thicker at one end than the other, and finished with a blob of clay at the thicker end which eventually became the bowl.

The pipe in its basic form was then put into a copper mould made in two halves. An instrument not unlike a conductor's baton, ending in a short upward curve, was placed along the stem of the mould to form the air passage, and the two halves of the mould clamped together. The inside of the bowl was then hollowed out through the open end of the mould, using a tool shaped like a small egg on a handle, and the connection between bowl and stem made with a wire. When the pipe had been taken out of the mould it was dried, the stem bent to the required curve, and fired at a low heat in small kilns.

This method was in use, with slight modifications, throughout the

Clay pipe bowl making machine

whole period of the popularity of clay pipes – until well into the nineteenth century in fact. The simple metal tools described required frequent replacement. Multiple pipe moulds may be found, the two halves hinged together and opening like a book. A form of 'do-it-yourself' pipe-making machine was produced in the middle of the nineteenth century. This simple affair consisted of a mould for the pipe-bowl, in two halves fixed vertically on a base board, one half clamping against the other after the clay was inserted, by means of a screw thread. The bowl was formed by pulling down a lever so that a shaped projection fixed to it was forced into the clay in the mould. The airway from the bottom of the bowl was probably made with a shaped wire after the mould had been unscrewed. The finished bowl, after it had been fired, was fitted with a stem of another material. The whole machine was not more than about a foot long, and must have produced crude but perfectly smokeable pipes.

Pipe Cases

A clay pipe was regarded as expendable, and was cheap in proportion (in 1650 they cost about 1½d each; by 1700 only about 2d a *dozen*). However, if one was travelling, or even out for the day, it was no answer to carry half-a-dozen clays with one as spares. The remedy was to carry the clay pipe in a pipe case. Sir Walter Raleigh, closely though probably mistakenly associated with the introduction of tobacco to this country, kept his pipe in a leather case. From the earliest days of smoking, some fine cases were produced, usually in wood. It was difficult (and in England at least regarded as scarcely worth the trouble) to decorate a clay pipe, but many cases made up this deficiency. On the whole English pipe-cases in wood are much simpler affairs than those made on the Continent. A common type was simply hollowed out from birch or sycamore like a dugout canoe, and for this reason had little aesthetic appeal as a keepsake.

Pipe cases are always more or less pipe-shaped in themselves, and the length of the stem and the angle and size of the 'bowl' are all closely allied to those changes in fashion of clay pipes themselves which have already been described.

The most elaborate English cases are those from the seventeenth century. They are often heavily carved and follow the small, forward-tilted shape of the pipe bowl characteristic of the period. Cases at this time were almost invariably made with a tapered sliding panel running the full length of the underside of the case, so that the top of the pipe bowl entered its case first.

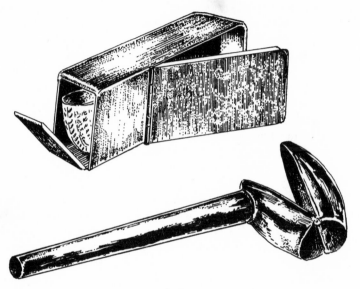

Metal pipe cases

In the succeeding century and afterwards, most clay pipe cases had a hinged lid forming half of the 'bowl', and the pipe was put in stem first. The main reason for this radical change in a perfectly satisfactory design was that after about 1700, clay pipes began to be made with a spur projecting from the bottom of the bowl, instead of the flat 'heel' common before this time. The spur kept the hot bowl of long-stemmed pipes off the table, but also made it impossible to close the sliding shutter of its case.

Many amusing designs were carved into Georgian and later pipe cases, often incorporating the bowl case as a human head. One notable eighteenth century example in the Pinto collection is even provided with a combination lock, so that no one but the owner could use the pipe inside.

Some particularly fine wooden cases were made by the Dutch. Fairholt illustrates a case said to have belonged to Admiral Van Tromp, and made of mahogany inlaid with brass. Mention is made elsewhere of pipe cases incorporated into tobacco boxes, particularly oblong brass boxes (which are more often than not Dutch in origin).

Tobacco Stoppers

Tobacco stoppers, which served the useful purpose of pressing down the burning tobacco in a pipe, and prickers, for removing caked ash from the sides and bottom of the pipe, went almost completely out of fashion in the middle of the nineteenth century. They have to some extent reappeared in favour during the present century, but most of the modern ones are purely utilitarian devices in cold and unadorned metal, and have none of the amusing charm of the originals.

Stoppers were certainly used in the seventeenth century, (in the early part of which a gentleman smoking in a tobacco-house was accustomed to have a boy waiting to keep his pipe properly trimmed for him), and although nothing more than a short cylinder, like a pencil stub, was needed to fit into the bowl of the pipe, they were usually

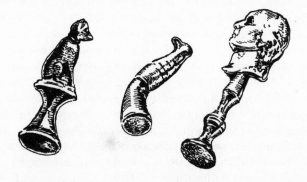

Pipe stoppers

turned into miniature works of art from the first. In the Wallace collection there is a tobacco stopper made of bone, carved into the shape of a finger. This, together with the red leather pouch of clay pipes and the gilded leather tobacco-box case which accompany it, are said to have belonged to Sir Walter Raleigh.

Seventeenth century stoppers are recognisable from later examples by the diameter of the operative part. In order to be able to fit into the very small pipe bowls characteristic of the period, the stopper itself was made less than half-an-inch in diameter. As a general rule, anything wider than this belongs to the eighteenth century or later. Pipe stoppers were meant to be carried in the pocket, and are seldom longer than about four inches. Most, in fact, are about half this length. Designs are very varied. A little work called *Paper of Tobacco*, published anonymously in 1839, is quoted by Fairholt as follows: 'This was the only article on which the English smoker prided himself. It was made of various materials – wood, bone, ivory, mother-of-pearl, and silver; and the forms which it assumed were exceedingly diversified. Out of a collection of upwards of thirty tobacco-stoppers of different ages, from 1688 to the present time, the following are the most remarkable: a bear's tooth tipped with silver at the bottom, and inscribed with the name of Captain James Rogers of the Happy Return Whaler, 1688; Dr Henry Sacheverel in full canonicals carved in ivory, 1710; a boot, a horse's hind leg, Punch and another character in the same Drama, to wit, his Satanic majesty; a countryman with a flail; a milkmaid, an emblem of Priapus, a bottle, Hope and Anchor, the Marquis of Granby, a greyhound's head and neck, a paviour's rammer, Lord Nelson, the Duke of Wellington, and Buonaparte'.

Probably the most common are those carved from wood, because they were the easiest for a reasonably handy man to make himself. Any wood would do, but of course the harder and less combustible it was, the longer would the stopper last, as its whole purpose in life was to be brought into contact with burning tobacco. Popular too, and sure of a ready market, were the stoppers made from historic wood – oak from a famous old naval vessel now broken up; or from the oak-tree at Boscobel in which King Charles hid from Cromwell's soldiers (there are enough articles made in wood attributed to this source to stock a fair-sized forest); or mulberry from Shakespeare's tree. Other materials suitable for carving which were used for making pipe stoppers included ivory, bone and horn. The quality of carving varies enormously as one might expect, and the finished articles range from the crudest of home-made examples to specimens of great beauty and intricate detail. It was common for the decorative part of the stopper to be carved above the utilitarian little pillar, which did the actual work; the carving acted as a handle, and was kept away from damage by the stopper itself. In some of the better examples, the bottom of the stopper was capped in metal – silver or pewter as a rule – to prevent charring.

Among subjects, human figures, heads and animals are probably the most frequently seen. Natural examples of strange growths, such as gnarled roots or burrs, or twisted horns, were popular during that part of the Victorian era when the grotesque was fashionable (though they were by no means unknown in the preceding century). One highly popular subject, which remained in fashion throughout the whole period of the pipe-stopper, was the miniature human arm or (more often) leg. The leg is typically bent at the knee, is obviously female and usually wears a garter at the knee. It was a slightly risqué joke which remained evergreen for generation after generation of smokers.

The leg, and many other simple designs, were made wholesale in metal during the eighteenth and nineteenth centuries, and a good many have been reproduced since. Brass was the commonest metal for both originals and reproductions, but pewter, bronze and silver were also used – as no doubt were iron, lead and other metals too. Some exquisite examples in pottery and porcelain were also produced in the same period, and pipe stoppers in glass, and even mother-of-pearl, are known.

Particular mention should be made of *'memento mori'* stoppers, carved with symbols of death and mourning; of stoppers carved in the same way as some of the famous Welsh 'love-spoons', so that a wooden ball is trapped inside a cage in the handle, the whole carved from a single piece of wood; and of a now rare type of stopper incorporated into a finger ring. This was not uncommon in the eighteenth century—Hogarth pictures a clergyman wearing one in his 'Modern Midnight Conversation'.

Tobacco Prickers

As with many of the bygones connected with tobacco, it was not unusual for two items useful to the pipe-smoker to be incorporated into a single design. The collector may find a pipe-stopper combined with a pricker to free caked tobacco. Sometimes the pricker is contained in the shaft of the stopper, and is withdrawn by removing one end. Less often it is part of the design of the pipe stopper, which is then less convenient to carry in the pocket. Prickers were made individually too – steel bodkins capped with a wooden or metal knob as a handle, and kept in a pencil-shaped case; or for the dedicated, carved bone points.

Finally, most briar smokers demanded a blade to scrape the inside of the bowl free of carbonisation. The pen-knife, as the need for cutting quill pens disappeared during the nineteenth century, was adapted for this purpose in many cases, but some complete outfits containing stopper, pricker and scraper were produced in metal towards the end of the century, so that the proud owner could never be caught without the appropriate tool.

Tobacco Cutters

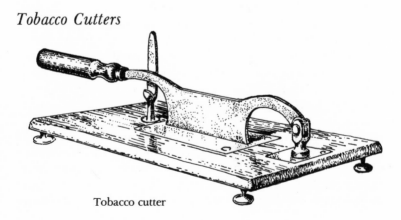

Tobacco cutter

In the days when one bought one's tobacco in the form of a hard twist or roll, it was necessary to have a sharp instrument to cut off what one needed, and then to rub it into flakes fit to be packed into the pipe. Most people used a pocket knife, but some kept a special tobacco-cutter for the purpose. They were probably used in tobacco-shops more than in private houses. The tobacco cutter is a steel blade of unmistakeable shape, hinged at one end to an upright swivel pin fixed into a heavy block of wood, and provided with a wooden handle at the other. The cutting part of the blade is three or four inches long as a rule, and is absolutely flat, fitting closely to the surface of the wooden base; it then rises in an arc to the handle, so that the user's fingers will not be trapped against the base. The wooden block is usually of maple, although more elegant examples were made in the Regency period using mahogany and brass.

Semi-automatic tobacco cutter of 1870

A more handsome and complicated tobacco-cutter was made in about 1870. This, of brass and mahogany, was semi-automatic, for the action of working the cutting blade up and down moved the plug of tobacco forward by means of a train of gears. The cut slices fell into a sliding tray.

4. Tobacco Jars and Boxes

The word 'jar' perhaps gives to the modern ear the idea of glass or pottery. Although pottery containers were certainly used for holding cut tobacco, a tobacco jar to the collector is a receptacle of any material intended to store tobacco in the house or the shop. As a rule, tobacco jars have detachable lids, and they are normally taller than they are wide or long. A tobacco box on the other hand was intended to be portable, and has a tight-fitting hinged lid. By its very nature it is flat, to fit the pocket. The only type of tobacco box which does not follow all these characteristics is the tavern box, which will be mentioned later.

Even if Sir Walter Raleigh may not have been the bringer of tobacco to this country, his name remains firmly linked with the event, and the story of how his servant, thinking his master was on fire, threw a jug of ale over him when he was smoking is certainly the best-known in the repertoire of tobacco folk-lore. It is not therefore surprising to find this scene decorating the side of a lead tobacco jar of the nineteenth century.

This is only one of innumerable themes which were used to embellish jars for holding tobacco in the home.

Lead Jars

By far the most commonly-used material for tobacco jars was lead, and from the second half of the seventeenth century until the end of the nineteenth, an enormous number were made in this metal. The reason for lead as the basis is not very clear when one considers the

Lead tobacco jar with impressed smoking scene

many other materials available. Its chief merit for the purpose is that it is a poor conductor of heat, so that the contents remain at a fairly even temperature.

The earliest lead jars (dating from about 1660) were generally cylindrical in shape. The most familiar shape to collectors, however, is the octagonal – or rather oblong with cut-off corners – jar, which appeared towards the end of the eighteenth century. Decorative plinths are quite common, and the lid is normally domed to a finial. The size is usually about six inches by five inches in height.

Lead jars of this kind were cast from carved wooden panels, and one would expect from this method of production that large numbers of identical jars, all cast from the same mould, would be found. In practice, the reverse is true – almost every jar seems to be decorated with a different theme of design. We can therefore only indicate the broad divisions of subject-matter in the decorative castings.

Understandably, the theme of tobacco itself is one of the commonest – crossed tobacco pipes, or a portrait of a man smoking, for example. Also relatively common is a combination of smoking and drinking themes, for many of these rather crude containers were made for the inns of nineteenth century England.

A favourite device was the commemoration of some national event. Among events of the early nineteenth century which were recorded in lead in this way were the Act of Union in 1801, the start of the Regency in 1811 and the Peace of 1814. The end of the Crimean War in 1856 was marked with an ornate lead jar showing the names of the main battles – Alma, Sebastopol, Balaclava and Inkerman – cast in the lid, and martial scenes round the sides. This particular jar, as is the case with almost all lead jars of the nineteenth century, was originally painted in bright colours. The colours were gaudy as a rule – reds, yellows, greens and purples predominate. Unfortunately, jars with their paintwork still in the original condition are virtually unknown, even where they were made no more than about sixty years ago. The soft lead does not provide the rigid base which would have preserved the paint.

Probably the commonest lead jar of all is plain except for some swags cast round the top and bottom. The central area is painted, the design and colours varying from jar to jar. The lid is domed, and the knob is a negro's head painted in black (the negro's head as a tobacco symbol was in use as a knob for the jar as early as 1617, according to Richard Braithwaite's *Smoaking Age* published in that year).

Although the Dutch also made them, and to some extent the French, lead tobacco jars were very largely an English production. It is practically impossible to date specific jars, except in the rare cases where the style or decorative theme is identifiable because of its similarity with contemporary products in other materials; even then, the way is strewn with pitfalls, for it was by no means uncommon in the nineteenth century for moulds of up to a hundred years earlier to be used to cast the panels for late Victorian tobacco jars.

It is equally rare to be able to identify the maker, for very seldom did a maker either sign or date his products. With the exception of

Oval lead tobacco jar

Stephen Loveless of Norwich, who marked a few of his jars, and Robert Howard, a tin-plate worker and brazier who worked at the sign of the Wheatsheaf and Trumpet in Smithfield towards the end of the nineteenth century, the makers are practically unknown.

Howard's address, however, gives a clue to some of the not uncommon decorative schemes on lead jars which might otherwise be difficult to explain – designs such as the wheatsheaf, or the spread eagle, the crown and the dolphin. These were all shop or inn signs of the eighteenth century. Many tradesmen marked their premises in this way to make them easily recognisable by their largely illiterate customers. It is very likely that inns and shops should have their tobacco jars marked with their own signs.

Another popular decorative theme on lead tobacco jars was sport in all its eighteenth and early nineteenth century ramifications – which ranged from cards through fox-hunting, shooting and fishing to tiger hunting. One jar illustrated in Mr Reginald Myer's work *Chats on Old English Tobacco Jars* shows the strange combination of tiger-hunting scenes on the sides and a bust of Shakespeare as the knob of the lid. It is likely that the knob was a later replacement (this often happens), and Mr Myers conjectures that the box was originally made for an official of the East India Company, that immensely powerful trading organisation whose fingers probed deep into every facet of India, including its government, between 1601 and 1858. The problem of keeping tobacco cool and moist (this was, and is, the English taste; the French on the other hand have always liked theirs hot and dry) was considerable in the climate of India, and many lead jars must have found their way there in military or Company hands.

For the reasons given above, the dating of jars by the subject-matter of the decorations on the panels is a risky affair. A slightly more trustworthy way is by the style. A good example of this lies in the

Tobacco jar in Gothic style

monstrous (or not, according to your taste) and quite unmistakeable products of the Gothic Revival period, which ran from about 1790 to about 1830). 'Gothick' lead jars express themselves not only in the familiar arches and medieval themes, but also in a morbid affection for church furnishings. So we find jars in the form of fonts and pulpits, jars decorated with pointed windows filled with mirror glass or quatrefoil windows in mock stonework, even jars in the shape of tombs and sarcophagi, complete with emblems of death in light relief. 'Steeple Jars' were also popular at this period. The jars themselves are square or round, usually with a projecting flange as a foot and a matching flange at the top of the body of the jar, but otherwise very plain. The 'steeple' is formed by the lid, which rises to a point topped with a decorated knob. The lid is often taller than the box itself.

Some of the decorations on lead tobacco jars would seem to indicate that they were made specially for the export market. Washington and Napoleon both appear as finials to the lid. Napoleon indeed was quite a popular subject in this medium; most of these jars were produced after his death in 1821.

Among other regular themes appearing in the cast sides of lead jars are agricultural symbols (the horn of plenty was popular), and masonic emblems.

Another type of lead jar relied for its decorations on separate lead castings soldered to the sides of the jar, which was otherwise plain. The castings usually consist of swags of foliage or some other stylised pattern at the top and bottom of the jar, with a single symbol set in the middle of each side – a lion's head, or an eagle, or a crown, all probably taken from trade signs as indicated above. More ornate and ambitious castings were applied in some cases, groups of children, country and sporting scenes being popular.

Many materials other than lead were also used for tobacco-jars.

Cast iron was not uncommon, the general shapes and decorative themes following very much the pattern of cast lead jars. Indeed, lead and cast iron jars, identical in design and decorations, are recorded. Cast iron was used particularly for jars made in the Gothic revival period at the beginning of the nineteenth century.

Pewter Jars

Pewter was probably used more than any other material after lead, and it is likely that some of the very earliest jars (from the sixteenth century) were made in this material, which has many of the characteristics of lead – which is of course its main ingredient. Pewter has, however, the advantage over lead of taking an attractive polish. For this reason, a large proportion of pewter tobacco jars rely on their shape, and on their unembellished lustrous surface for decoration. Late eighteenth century examples in pewter are the only tobacco jars which can truly be described as beautiful, with their simple designs based on silver-work of the same period. In general, the standard of craftsmanship was considerably higher in pewter jars than it was in lead ones, and details such as the finial to the lid are often minor works of art. It must be remembered, in fairness, that the casting of lead in carved wooden moulds was a simple enough craft for it to have developed into what was almost a cottage industry; some lead jars are crude in the extreme.

Pewter jars in the familiar octagonal shape were also made, and painted with stylised designs on the flat, unmoulded sides.

Wooden Jars

A non-smoker might think that of all materials, wood should be the most suitable, as well as the cheapest, material for tobacco-jars. If cheapness were the only factor, this would be true. But as we have already seen, it is not liked by tobacco addicts because it tends to allow the contents to dry out. None the less, very many wooden jars have been made. Fairholt describes a wooden jar (or rather box), traditionally said to have belonged to Sir Walter Raleigh. This is coffin-shaped with a sliding lid, and is covered with carvings of men and women in late sixteenth or early seventeenth century costume. On the bottom of the box is a compass, and inside the lid are carved the initials W.R.

Wooden jars can vary from crude home-made containers, often carved from a single piece of wood, to elegant affairs of turned mahogany decorated with bands of silver, made very largely at the end of the eighteenth century. It has been pointed out by Mr Edward Pinto, whose collection of bygone wooden objects is unsurpassed in the world, that eighteenth century wooden tobacco jars are often confused with small tea-caddies of the same period, and that a generally reliable way of separating them is by remembering that tea-caddies usually had locks, tea being at that time an expensive luxury.

A not uncommon way for makers to use the attractiveness of a wooden box and still provide a container which would keep the tobacco in good condition was for a lead (or more rarely, copper or zinc) lining to be fitted to the inside.

One eighteenth century novelty which the collector might come across is the wooden tobacco jar in the form of a negro's head. This was a popular symbol for tobacco, and will be met again in the chapter dealing with snuff. These negro's head boxes have been reproduced in modern times. Another popular curiosity in the nineteenth century was the tobacco jar of bog-oak, that semi-fossilised and almost steel-hard wood occasionally dug up out of marshy ground.

Pottery Jars

Pottery is one of the commonest materials for modern mass-produced tobacco-jars; its cheapness made it popular from the early days of smoking. The Fulham and Isleworth potteries (among others) produced considerable quantities towards the end of the eighteenth century. They were usually round with slightly domed lids, and came in a wide variety of colours and decorative schemes. Moulded decorations showing sporting scenes and aspects of smoking were popular. Not a few jars of classical Wedgwood type were made by various Staffordshire potteries, the background in plain colours and the applied moulded scenes or figures in white.

Pottery jars vary enormously, even when the products of England alone are considered. There was also a large volume of examples from foreign (mainly German) potteries which arrived here during the nineteenth century. As few potters signed their wares, the collector has a wide and nebulous field to lose himself in. One rather attractive design in stoneware clay, formed in the shape of a barrel, was intended to represent a tobacco-cask rather than a beer or spirits barrel. The removable lid distinguishes the tobacco jar from the otherwise very similar stoneware spirit flask sold in taverns in the early nineteenth century.

Martinware tobacco jar

Outstanding among pottery tobacco jars of recent times are the few made by the Martin brothers between 1873 and the beginning of the 1914-18 War. The Martin brothers worked in various parts of London, producing a wide range of containers modelled in stoneware clay – not only jugs, jars and bowls, but candlesticks, windowboxes, even umbrella stands. Every single piece was individually modelled, and no two are alike. Each piece is signed. One of the best-known of their products is a tobacco-jar in the form of an owl, the head of which forms the lid.

Before leaving the subject of tobacco jars, mention should be made of the pressers which were normally part of every jar. Whatever material the jar itself might be made of, the presser was usually lead, so that its weight would do the required job of keeping the tobacco compacted (which helped to stop it drying out). Tobacco pressers in their basic form were simple flat lead plates, cut to the same shape as the parent box, and of such a size to fit reasonably closely into it. The centre of the presser was fitted with a knob for lifting. Just as the lid of the jar itself was often finished in a decorative finial, so the presser's lifting handle was usually fashioned into something more interesting than a plain button. The theme of the decoration on the outside of the jar was often repeated on the presser. Where a jar and its presser show any considerable difference in decorative themes, it usually means that they are strangers to each other.

Brass Jars

Brass jars, usually of neo-Gothic form and relying largely on the sheen of polished metal for their appeal, were made in some numbers in the early nineteenth century, both in this country and in Holland.

Brass Boxes

Brass was also the favourite material for tobacco-boxes, the portable containers which a man carried round in his pocket and refilled at home from his tobacco-jar. These were made earlier than tobacco jars. Thomas Dekker, in his *Gull's Horn Book of 1602*, talks of the gallant with his tobacco box; a small and handsome tobacco box, carried by a lady smoker, is illustrated in a portrait of 1650.

The traditional Dutch box was introduced in the seventeenth century and copied in England afterwards. A typical box of this type is made in heavy brass, and measures some six inches long, two inches wide and one inch high. The lid is normally hinged on one long side, and covered with hand-engraving which has a refreshing lack of sophistication. Common subjects are such things as country scenes, flying birds, shooting adventures and landscapes with figures – or, again, smoking and drinking scenes.

Biblical subjects were frequently engraved, one of the most usual being Noah and the Flood; other themes to be found are famous battles and historical portraits. Some of these boxes instead of being engraved are embossed from inside the lid. Oval and square boxes of the same type were also made in brass and some were made in copper.

There are examples of seventeenth century Dutch boxes in the Guildhall Museum in London where the sides are made of copper and the lids of brass – a combination which is very pleasing to the eye. The simple engraving which was such an attractive feature of these early Dutch boxes gave way at the end of the eighteenth century to much stiffer and more formal work – scrolls and medallions and ornamented borders.

One other type of oblong brass tobacco box which should be mentioned is large enough to hold a clay pipe as well as the tobacco. The pipe lies behind a hinged lid at the end of the box, and the tobacco in a small compartment at the opposite end. Some boxes of this kind were provided with extra compartments to hold flint and steel also.

Steel Boxes

Steel pocket boxes of smaller size (some two inches square and very shallow) were made in this country in the late eighteenth and nineteenth centuries. Some are engraved, but many are quite plain. They were probably the cheapest form of portable tobacco box with any pretensions to quality, and were fitted with hinged lid and spring catch. A particularly attractive steel pocket box of the early nineteenth century, mentioned in Mr J. Seymour Lindsay's *Iron and Brass Implements of the English House* as being in the collection of Mr C. M. Escare, shows a negro sitting smoking on a barrel. On one side is a tropical scene, with bales of tobacco, palm trees and a ship at sea; on the other, the entrance to a house (or more probably a shop). Round the lid is engraved 'My Massa Sells de Best Tobacco'. This was obviously an advertisement box, and would have been sold in the tobacconist's shop.

Mechanical Boxes

The generosity implied in the painted inscription on the back of one of Mr Myer's lead jars:-

WELCOME

FRIEND

TO FILL

was by no means universal. Not every host liked all comers to help themselves from his tobacco jar or box. Still less was this true where the host kept an inn, and an ingenious mechanical box in brass was made in the eighteenth century to ensure that the smoker paid for what he took. This was a perfectly plain oblong box, about twelve inches long, six inches wide and six inches deep, divided into two compartments each with a separate lid, and with a carrying handle in the centre. One side of the box was a container for tobacco, the other a penny (or sometimes halfpenny) in the slot mechanism. The customer put in his penny and struck a projecting knob. The lid of the other compartment flew open, and he helped himself. The customer had to be trusted to take no more than a pennyworth 'fill' for his pipe, and also to close the lid of the box before all his friends helped themselves too. It seems to have been the custom, according to a rhyme engraved on one box, for anyone who forgot to close the lid to pay a fine of sixpence. This box is labelled 'Rich's Patent' and is probably of late eighteenth century vintage.

A certain S. Stocker took out a patent in 1849 for 'Improvements in Tobacco Boxes, used by Publicans'. This was a rather cumbersome clock-shaped machine, which did not prove popular.

A Special Box

The last tobacco-box we shall describe is quite unique. It is made of horn, similar to the Scottish pocket snuff boxes used by every cottager in the eighteenth century. It was originally bought at the Horn Fair at Charlton, in Kent, for the sum of 4d by Henry Monck, one of the Overseers of the Parish of St Margaret and St John in Westminster. It was presented by Monck in 1713 to the Society of Past Overseers (made up of these officials after their year of office was over). They decided that it should become a treasured possession of their Society, and that every overseer, when his official year was over, should attach a silver plate to the box commemorating the chief event in the history of the country during that year. As time went by, space on the little box ran out. As the silver plates multiplied, a new outer case was added to contain the box, and then a case to hold the first case, and so on. The box and its many cases now provides a unique record of the history of England through a period of two and a half centuries.

5. *Striking a Light*

The man who lights his pipe from the flame of a butane gas lighter in the teeth of a wet north-east gale, or the man who presses his cigar against the glowing element in the dashboard of his car as he speeds along the motorway, has little idea of the frustrations that science has

Tinder box combined with candlestand

saved him from. For centuries after the introduction of tobacco, the only way in which a smoker could produce a light for his pipe was by means of a flint and steel. There was little difficulty in striking a spark from these two articles, but the art lay in persuading the spark to set alight the tinder which was carried with them. Tinder could be made of almost any inflammable material. The cheapest, and most common, was charred rags. Under favourable conditions, the user could persuade good, dry tinder to burst into flame without much difficulty, although one writer in 1832 after conducting 'many thousands of experiments' came to the conclusion that 'There are very few house-men, or house-maids, who can succeed in striking-a-light in less than three minutes'. When the conditions were not ideal, there were additional hazards – 'On a cold, dark frosty morning when the hands are chapped, frozen and insensible, you may chance to strike the flint against your knuckles for some considerable time without discovering your mistake'.

Another favourite sort of tinder was *amadou*, a kind of fungus which dry-fly fishermen will recognise as an ally in their own special field – (it is used for drying the water from an artificial fly). Amadou and other forms of tinder were often impregnated with an inflammable chemical such as saltpetre or sulphur to help the sparks from the steel gain a firm hold. Amadou in a specially prepared form was called 'German tinder' and was sometimes hardened and used for the stems of early friction matches.

Steels and tinder boxes take many forms. The flint, used for the very reason that it is harder than steel (it is the steel which produces the sparks when the two are struck together), remains a flint.

Steels

The steel in its basic form is no more than a flat bar some three or four inches long and up to an inch wide. This unelaborate form was extremely difficult to manipulate, however; for the way to use a flint and steel is to hold the flint between the finger and thumb of one hand, and to strike it against the long edge of the steel held in the other. If the reader will try this with a flat bar of steel, the reason for a rapid modification in design will be clear. The new design was certainly in use in the sixteenth century, and probably much earlier. It required no more than the extension of the bar at one or both ends, so that the sides wrapped round the fingers, providing both a handle and a guard. In some steels the extension is carried right round from one end to the other, forming a loop handle.

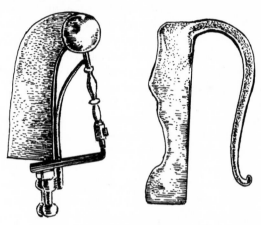

Two types of steel

The flat bar, with or without hand-guards, was the simplest type of steel. This is what the soldier, the farm-labourer, and the maid servant used to produce a spark. They can occasionally be found worn away almost to nothing, showing the constant use to which they were put. The flat steel surface lent itself well to chased decoration, however, and steels of the same basic pattern are to be found bearing names, dates, slogans or scenes cut into the metal. Particularly richly-decorated are some of the steels made in Spain and the near East during the sixteenth and seventeenth centuries. The metal is sometimes cut into the shape of a bird or animal, and appropriate decorations hand-chased upon the side. The really rich had their steels set with precious stones.

In this country, it was more common for elaboration to be achieved not by decorating the steel itself, but by setting the steel into some other object – usually, for obvious reasons, a tinder box – which could be made attractive.

Tinder Boxes

The tinder box began by being a purely utilitarian container, whose only functions were to hold the flint, steel and tinder and to keep the tinder dry when it was not required; and to be reasonably flame-proof when it was in action. A common cottage design was made in wood, and looked like a square miniature frying-pan with a lid. It hung on the wall from a loop at the end of the handle when not in use. The inside of a wooden tinder-box will invariably show signs of charring, even if scraps of tinder are not still there, as they often are, to help the identification.

In the eighteenth and early nineteenth centuries, tinder boxes were often made in metal; pewter was common. Most were round, and without their lids look much like a flat cup. A lid is an essential part of a tinder-box, however, and many also had an additional inner lid, which could be pressed down on to the glowing tinder to extinguish it after the fire had been transferred to one's pipe. An added refinement which is not uncommon on Georgian tinder-boxes is a candle-socket

Cottage tinder box

set in the lid. Like the steels which went with them, some of the personal tinder-boxes belonging to wealthy smokers were richly decorated with inlays of gold and silver, or encrusted with jewels. This is particularly true of early seventeenth century examples.

Pocket Tinder Boxes

The boxes so far described were for use in the home, and were too large to be carried about. Pocket tinder boxes, usually complete with a steel set in the side or end, were also made in the same period, and are often extremely handsome. Silver and pewter are seen more frequently than other materials, and decorative themes are as varied as they are on their cousins, the snuff boxes of similar materials. Pocket tinder boxes are necessarily small, and contain sufficient tinder only for a day's use.

Tinder Horns

If one was travelling, a common means of producing a light in Stuart times was the tinder-horn. This was basically a hollowed-out cow's horn fitted with a stopper and hangers so that it could be carried at the belt. Inside was the usual equipment of flint, steel and tinder. These horns too were often richly decorated with exquisite carvings or inlay.

Tinder Pouches

The countryman and the labourer kept his flint, steel and tinder in a simple leather bag. Few of these utilitarian containers have survived, even though their history goes back for many hundreds of years. Some tinder bags from the seventeenth century were works of art in themselves, in tapestry, or tooled and gilded leather, or rare animal skins. Elaborate examples of the tinder pouch are known, particularly from the late eighteenth and early nineteenth centuries, where the bag is made of cloth, embroidered or decorated with beadwork, and the steel is permanently attached to the bottom.

Tinder pouch

Sulphur Matches

A pipe of tobacco was normally lit from a candle or from a glowing coal removed from the fire with special tongs, for the glowing tinder which had been successfully produced from flint and steel was only the first stage in the achievement of the steady, untainted flame that the smoker wanted. To produce sufficient heat to light the candle itself, another intermediary was needed. For centuries (even from the time of the Romans) until the introduction of the first friction matches, this intermediary was the sulphur match – a splinter of dry wood tipped at one end with a blob of sulphur. Manufactured

Sulphur matches and holder

sulphur matches of the eighteenth century were usually substantial affairs – about six inches long and an inch wide, sharpened to a point and tipped with sulphur at each end. They produced a clear and steady flame when the sulphur was put into the glowing tinder, but the fumes were not only evil-smelling but actively dangerous; and anyone who lit his pipe direct from a sulphur match spent the first dozen puffs trying to get rid of the taste.

Mechanical Tinder Boxes

The principle of producing a spark from a flint striking a steel was used early in the history of firearms, taking the place of the glowing torch which had been applied to a touch-hole filled with gunpowder. The flint-lock and wheel-lock mechanisms for producing a spark to ignite the powder appeared during the first half of the sixteenth century, and it was not long before the devices were incorporated into tinder boxes. These mechanical tinder boxes are now very rare, and their discovery outside a museum would be a collector's triumph. The mechanism is usually crude and heavy, and is fixed to the outside of a wooden box. More delicate affairs were certainly produced in the sixteenth and seventeenth centuries, but these are correspondingly even rarer.

Tinder Pistols

Developing from the mechanical tinder box, many ingenious and decorative tinder pistols were made during the seventeenth and early eighteenth centuries. Most of them were designed to stand on a table. Some of these, and particularly the earlier examples, were so cleverly disguised that they can easily be mistaken for real pistols, and many were indeed converted from them. In this type, there is usually a folding iron strut under the barrel, which enables the pistol to be stood upright. The spark was produced by pulling the trigger, when the flint sprang forward to strike the steel in the normal way. A small charge of gunpowder was ignited, and transferred its flame to a piece of amadou held in a socket inside the barrel. The barrel of the pistol was cut in half longitudinally and hinged on one side; the hinged barrel opened and the amadou-socket sprang up, holding its burning contents ready for the pipe.

Another form of tinder pistol made in the early eighteenth century was less ingenious, but perhaps more certain in its action. This had no barrel, and the hammer sent its spark into an open container for tinder. The final flame was produced by holding a sulphur match to the smouldering tinder, as in the normal household tinder box. In some examples, the pistol-shape disappeared entirely,

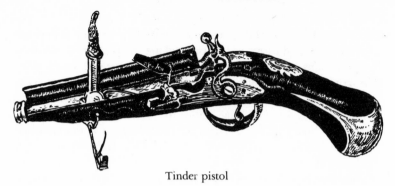

Tinder pistol

a turned handle was incorporated to hold the mechanism steady
while the trigger was operated, and the whole 'pistol' was mounted
on a shaft and foot. In others, where the pistol shape was retained,
the butt folds back at the touch of a spring-catch, to disclose a
container for holding a supply of tinder and sulphur matches.

Tinder pistols were sometimes incorporated into other household
pieces. Particularly useful was the combined tinder pistol, inkwell and
adjustable candle-stand, which allowed a correspondent to write his
letter and seal it with wax after lighting the candle from the pistol.
But surely the most ingenious of the tinder-pistol combinations was
the early eighteenth century alarm clock, which as it reached the pre-
set time not only rang a bell, but also set off a chain of events which
resulted in a lighted candle springing from the clock housing.
Certainly the twentieth century has no cause to feel self-satisfied over
the invention of the automatic tea-making clock.

Fire-Pistons

Another ingenious device for persuading tinder to ignite made use
of a completely different principle. The fire-piston, patented in
England in 1807, was regarded at the time as a new break-through in
scientific research. In fact, it had been used for centuries in the area
of Burma and the Malayan peninsular, and some traveller doubtless
brought an example home with him. The fire-piston, or fire-syringe,

used the latent heat of compressed air to ignite the tinder. Anyone who has pumped up a bicycle tyre will know that the end of the pump gets hot. The fire piston was basically a bicycle-pump without a hole in the end. A small piece of tinder was fixed into the end of the piston, which was then fitted tightly into the tube. A sharp movement of the piston to the bottom of the closed tube usually produced enough heat to ignite the tinder, which was then withdrawn glowing into the open air. In this country, fire-pistons were usually made with a brass tube, and a brass piston fixed to a steel rod. The total length was up to about six inches (although the very first patent by Richard Lorentz in 1807 was for a 'fire-piston walking stick'). They were not used very widely, nor for very long – except by eccentrics.

Instantaneous Light Contrivances

In their search for an alternative method of producing a flame without the time-consuming, messy, elaborate and often unreliable flint, steel and tinder, the inventors of the late eighteenth and early nineteenth centuries came up with some remarkable devices. What the public wanted, and what many of the most able chemists of the Georgian era were trying to find, was an 'instantaneous light contrivance'. Some of the attempts were a good deal more dangerous than the sulphur match, the hazards of which have already been mentioned. In 1766, a Mr Hoppie advertised in London 'a newly invented phosphorus powder' for lighting pipes quickly in about half a minute. 'Ask', said Mr Hoppie, 'for a Bottle of Thunder Powder'! Another of the earliest devices, a French invention of 1786 which was taken up by a London maker about ten years later, used pure white phosphorus, a notoriously dangerous substance. The equipment was merely a glass bottle containing phosphorus, a bundle of match-sized tapers, and a cork, all in a small box, the hinged lid of which contained instruc- tions. One of the wooden tapers was to be dipped into the bottle and then rubbed on the cork, when the friction should cause the phosphor- us, and consequently the stick, to burst into flame. These matches were known as 'Pocket Luminaries'.

Much more certain, but just as dangerous and the cause of

numerous domestic accidents, was its successor, the Instantaneous Light Box. This was introduced (again from France) in about 1810 and used in most middle-class homes until the beginning of the Victorian era in 1837. There were many different patterns, but all made use of the same principle. The match heads were made of potassium chlorate and sugar, held together with a little gum. The only other necessary equipment was a glass bottle containing vitriol – concentrated sulphuric acid. The match head was dipped quickly into the bottle and would, nine times out of ten, burst into flame as it was withdrawn. Some care had to be taken by the manufacturers to make sure that the highly corrosive acid remained in the bottle and did not come into contact with the match heads except when this was intended. The danger was considerable, for many travelling boxes were made. Characteristically the tiny glass bottle is very narrow-necked, and the matches are held in a separate compartment. The lid is either spring

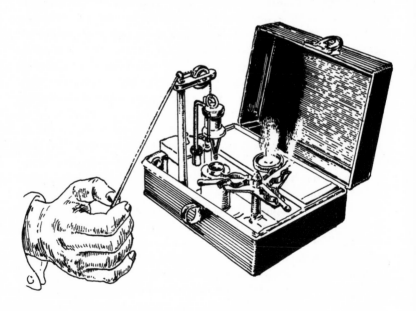

Instantaneous light contrivance

loaded (in the case of metal containers) with a pad which is held against the mouth of the bottle; or in the wooden containers the glass phial has a stopper, held in place by a screw-on lid which prevents the stopper from coming out of the mouth of the bottle. Some containers are circular, the compartments for bottle and matches being formed from two concentric rings. In others, there are compartments not only for these, but also for a candle; and incorporated in a hinged flap at one end of the metal box is a candle holder.

Some ingenious devices were developed to lessen the risks caused by the bottle of highly corrosive acid necessary for the use of these early matches. In 1824 Henry Berry, who remained at the forefront of development in lighting techniques for most of the first half of the nineteenth century, patented his own 'Instantaneous Light Box'. This device, which looked like a small japanned deed box when closed, was operated by pulling on a string. This one movement raised a glass stopper from the bottle of acid and allowed one drop to fall on a match head and, as the match caught fire, it moved in a rotating holder across the wick of a ready-primed spirit lamp. Releasing the string allowed the stopper to fall back into the bottle. This apparatus was specially designed for bedridden invalids, and probably killed more than one!

Burning Glasses

An ancient method of making a flame was brought up-to-date in the eighteenth century for the convenience of the smoker. Every boy has used a burning glass to focus the sun's rays for amusement, and the smoker sometimes found it a more convenient fire-raising device than any other. But he needed a sunny day to do it. Smokers' burning glasses were usually combined with some other piece of useful equipment – a pocket tobacco box, or a cigar holder, or a pipe-stopper. One example in the Bryant & May collection is combined with a fire-steel. Another looks like a pocket telescope in brass. It was made in two sections which slid into each other. At the outer end of one section was a holder for a piece of amadou. At the end of the other was the glass. The tube was pointed at the sun and the two halves

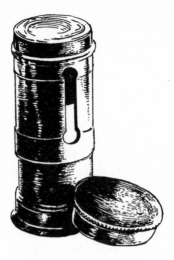

Burning-glass tinder box

adjusted until the focus of the glass fell on the tinder. As soon as this
was glowing, a sulphur match could be inserted through a slit in the
side.

Electro-Pneumatic Lamps

Of all the clever and complicated affairs intended to produce fire
with the minimum of effort, the most handsome and the most intricate was probably the Temple of Vesta, which was patented in this
country in 1807. It was only one of a class of similar machines known
as 'Electro-Pneumatic Lamps'. Concealed behind the collonades and
domes in mahogany and gilded metal was an apparatus for generating
hydrogen from the action of hydrochloric acid on zinc. In the base
was a disc of electro-phosphorus which could be charged with static
electricity by rubbing it with a piece of fur. This was necessary only
at infrequent intervals; the charge would hold for several weeks under
normal conditions of use. All the user had to do was to press a button
on the base. This released a spark in the path of a stream of hydrogen,

The Temple of Vesta

and a flame shot out of the mouth of a couchant lion at the door of the temple. Hydrogen is not the most reliable substance to deal with, and quite a few eyebrows must have been singed when the apparatus failed to spark at the first time of asking.

Promethean Matches

A development of the 'instantaneous light' was produced in 1828 by Samuel Jones of London. He called it the Promethean Match (nineteenth century inventors were very taken with the classics as a source of names for their products. Vesta, of course, was the Roman goddess of fire, and Prometheus stole fire from the gods. Lucifer, who appears shortly in this account, is literally 'Light-bearer'). The Promethean match still made use of acid, but it was now contained in a tiny sealed glass phial. Round this tube was wound a thin strip of paper which had been soaked in a mixture of potassium chlorate,

Prometheans and case

sugar and gum, and allowed to dry. To use the match, which was bought ready for operation in a handsome black and gold metal box, all that was needed was a pair of pliers. When the phial in its paper cover was nipped in the middle, the drop of acid met the chemicals in the paper, which burst into flame.

Friction Matches

The friction match, much as we know it today and one of the great inventions of the nineteenth cent ry, was first produced in 1827. The inventor was John Walker, a pharmacist of Stockton-on-Tees.

Walker's matches, which he called Friction Lights, were flat cardboard sticks tipped at one end with a mixture of potassium chlorate and antimony sulphide held together with gum. To light the match, the head was gripped in a piece of folded sandpaper and pulled smartly out. The original container for the Friction Lights was a cylindrical grey metal tin with a slip-on cap. A hundred matches cost one shilling, and the tin an extra twopence. A little later, the container became a cardboard box and the matches themselves wooden splints.

Walker's invention, which he did not patent, was pirated wholesale during the next few years without anyone producing a significant technical advance. Jones' 'Lucifers', (which rapidly became the generic name for matches) Watts' 'Chlorate Match' at 6d a hundred, and Bell's Lucifers were all very similar to Walker's product. It was at this time (about 1830) that matches began to be supplied in labelled cardboard or chip-board boxes similar to those in use today; the only difference was that the box was made with a detachable lid rather than the sliding tray and cover common to modern matches. And of course, each box was supplied with a separate piece of sandpaper in which the head of the match was gripped to produce the flame. By the early eighteen thirties, friction matches had virtually supplanted all other kinds of fire-producing devices.

Fuzees

In 1832, one of the few fire-making devices made specifically for the smoker was patented by Samuel Jones – the same who introduced the Promethean Match. This was the Fuzee, and it was obviously based on the slow-match, a kind of slowly-burning fuse kept permanently alight by the side of cannons in time of war. The Fuzee was usually made of thick cardboard or amadou, soaked in nitre – both of which would smoulder slowly and could not be blown out by the wind. They were supplied in strips about an inch and a half wide, divided in the same way as cardboard book-matches today, but into rather fatter 'matches'. Each Fuzee when required was torn off and the phosphorus-coated end struck against a sandpaper strip. Fuzees were supplied in sliding-tray cardboard boxes similar to, but larger than, a present-day matchbox. Some later Fuzees (about 1850-60) were scented.

Cigar Tips and Caps

From about 1845, a development of the Fuzee was made, mainly in Germany, for lighting cigars. These were known as Cigar Tips. The cheapest kind consisted of a large inflammable head on a short wooden stalk. The stalk was pushed into the end of the cigar and the head struck on the bottom of the box. Many of the better ones were disguised as flowers with a rosette of brightly coloured paper fixed round the head. 'Cigar Caps' also popular at about the same time, were cones of (usually) pink paper ending in a knob of inflammable material which was struck against the sandpaper on the box.

Cigar caps and tips

The instructions for one type of Cigar-Tips, 'Le Verrier's Newly-invented Planet Cegarlights', made in about 1845, reads as follows – 'Stick one of the lights into the centre of the end of the Cegar, rub it gently, against the rough part of the box, and begin to smoke as soon as it is lit! It will burn like a coal for five minutes and not cause any unpleasant smell or taste'.

Vesuvians

After the Fuzee came the Vesuvian, introduced by Palmer of Camberwell in 1849. The main feature of this was an enormous head, usually pear-shaped, and made up of sawdust, nitre, powdered charcoal and bark, all held together with gum; at the tip was the phosphorus striking surface. The Vesuvian was, at least in its early days, a monstrous thing. The head was designed to burn in the fiercest wind for about twenty seconds, so that a cigar or pipe could be well and truly lit. The first problem was that the wooden stem invariably burned through before the head had stopped flaming,

Box for Vesuvians

and one's clothes were often set on fire as the head fell. To overcome this, the head was fixed to a tube of glass or porcelain which would not burn through. The hazard then was that, as the head ignited, a flame was liable to shoot down the tube and up one's sleeve. However, the troubles were eventually overcome, and Vesuvians remained popular for the remainder of the century. Many different factories made them, and different safety devices were used to attach the head to the stem. Cotton braid and wire were common. They were known by such names as 'Flaming Fusees', 'Crystal Lights', 'Braided Lights', 'Cigar Lights' and 'Flamers'. One enterprising maker sold special matches of this kind for use by cyclists – for lighting lamps – which he called 'Velocipede Flamers'.

Congreves

Also in 1832 came the Congreve match. This was the first which could be struck anywhere, and the inventor was a Frenchman, Charles Sauria. In this country it was named after Sir William Congreve, the

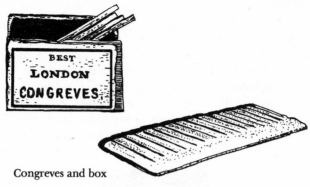

Congreves and box

rocket pioneer who had died in 1828. The main difference in appearance between Lucifers and these later Congreves was that Lucifers were considerably larger, as they required a good deal of force to persuade the mixture of which the head was made to burst into flame. The smaller Congreve, on the other hand, was almost too ready to do so. Congreves were usually round, unlike the flat Lucifers, and were generally covered in sulphur for up to a third of their length to help the quick flame of the phosphorus to gain a hold. Congreves, and the slightly later wax-stemmed Vestas (which were made by many different establishments, and which all contained some proportion of white phosphorus in the head) rapidly ousted the matches based on Walker's 'Friction Lights'. But they were too dangerous to carry loose in the pocket or in the usual flimsy wooden or cardboard boxes. As a result, between roughly 1830 and 1880 (when Congreves retired from the scene) an enormous number of containers, known as 'protective match boxes' or 'safety boxes', were made.

Early safety matchbox

Match Containers

As the only necessary features of such boxes were that they should be reasonably impervious to fire if the matches inside should ignite spontaneously; and that they should have somewhere about them a roughened surface (for the phosphorus match needed very little friction to set it off) every conceivable shape, pattern, material and decorative theme was used. One sometimes comes across a box which can be identified as a matchbox only by a ribbed or roughened area to serve as a striker. Some, and particularly the earlier ones, still made use of sandpaper for the striking surface. This was not supplied as a separate sheet, but was fixed to the bottom of the container. Often this sandpaper has gone with the passage of time, but as a rule the slight depression which was made at the bottom to hold the sand-paper, so that the edges would not catch, will inderitify the box as a match container.

Some idea of the danger of spontaneous combustion from these phosphorus matches can be had from the popularity of containers which held each individual match in a separate compartment. The most widely-used of these was Rush's 'Oxusophos', a green-painted metal box three inches high with a hinged lid, the inside of which was divided into eighty-one vertical compartments, each for one match. This was patented in 1842. Similar in intention is a wooden holder of about the same time, in shape not unlike a capstan. Matches were held horizontally, radiating out like the spokes of a wheel, and clamped firmly into place by the top disc.

Many pocket match containers were made in metal. A popular pattern was in the form of a miniature letter box, complete in every detail even to the times of collection, and painted in the traditional colour. The whole of the top lifts away from the base, which contains the matches. Underneath the base is a serrated striking surface, and at the top a holder for a single match, to allow for the sealing of a letter. This match was often called a 'go-to-bed' as it burned just long enough to allow one to get into bed after blowing out the candles.

Other 'disguised metal' cases were made in some quantity by Henry Berry. His speciality was leather-covered square boxes, usually embossed 'Light' in gold, opening on a hinge in the middle when a spring catch on the front is pressed. Inside the lid was a separate hinged plate, serrated to act as a striker. Berry and his successors and plagiarists also made travelling inkwells on the same principle, and where identical containers for matches and ink are found, it is likely that these formed part of a travelling writing case, and that the matches were largely for sealing letters rather than lighting a pipe or cigar.

Another popular shape was the miniature barrel, usually in lignum vitae. This attractive and highly-polished container unscrewed in the middle, and the striking surface was a disc of sandpaper recessed into one end. Tunbridge ware (and many cheap imitations of this delicate mosaic-like work on a wooden base) was used for match containers in the second half of the nineteenth century.

Wax Vestas, which were a good deal shorter than the usual modern match, were often kept in highly decorative little metal boxes, not infrequently of silver, designed to be hung from a watch-chain. These are to be found in surprising shapes, particularly those made as novelties at the very end of the Victorian period in about 1900 – bottles

Victorian matchboxes

Some attractive match containers

and violins, birds and fish, arms and legs. All are distinguished as matchboxes by the serrations of the striking surface, although some makers took a delight in disguising this too. The striking surface may be inside a secret spring-loaded flap, or, on the principle of not seeing the wood for the trees, some suitable shapes are completely covered with fine ridges.

At about the time of the Jubilee in 1887, many novelties made of a combination of ebony and ivory were put on the market, the popular shape being that of a crown. A small desk or table match-holder in this form opened by the crown being lifted from the base, to disclose a brass cylinder which not only held the matches but also acted as a striker by means of the rings engraved on its surface. Similar in style was a model mortar, in the wide mouth of which the Vestas were kept. The striking plate, of metal, was attached to the base.

In 1855, after a brief reign by the 'Strike-Anywhere' match (the head containing a type of phosphorus not liable to ignite spontaneously) the Safety Match was invented; and it has held sway ever since for domestic purposes. It works on the principle of separating the igniting material (phosphorus) from the burning composition (largely potassium chlorate) by having one in the match head and the other on a strip glued to the box. In this way, only by striking one against the other, and in no other circumstances, can a flame be produced. The 'safety' of the title also referred to the red phosphorus which was the main ingredient of the new composition. Red phosphorus, unlike the white variety it supplanted, held no medical dangers for the workers in the match factories.

Late nineteenth century silver matchbox holder

Lighters

An early attempt at producing a pocket lighter in France was notable mainly for its elegance. It was a cylindrical brass box about three inches high, containing another cylinder covered with *amorces* (a kind of percussion cap made largely of white phosphorus); this in turn held an iron pin wrapped with an impregnated tinder cord. The user had to scratch one of the *amorces* with the pin until it burst into flame and set fire to the tinder cord.

Equally unpredictable was a dangerous device brought out in France at about the same time (*c.* 1845). This was made up of two metal tubes joined together at the sides. One tube held the usual tinder cord, the other a spring-loaded plunger which came down on to an ordinary copper percussion-cap, as recently introduced in firearms of the time. As the percussion cap was struck, the flame shot through a hole in the side of the tube and set fire to the tinder cord.

One of the earliest devices which was obviously an ancestor of the modern pocket lighter was patented in 1851 (no doubt in time for the

Great Exhibition) in this country, probably from a German original. It was about four inches long, pencil shaped and made of brass. Inside the brass tube was a cord fuse made of wool impregnated with nitre. Fixed to the cord every inch or so was an *amorce*. To use the lighter, the top of the 'pencil' was taken off and the cord pulled up until the next *amorce* appeared. This was then rubbed against the rough sharkskin which covered the detachable top, until it burst into flame and set the cord smouldering. Similar in principle, but very different in appearance, was a later (1865) American patent. This was circular, an inch and a half across, with a flat top and bottom (a small drum in fact). On the side was fixed a nozzle with a chained cap, and a handle projecting from a miniature drum. When the cap was removed from the nozzle and the handle turned, an *amorce* in the nozzle, one of many on a long cotton tape coiled inside the main drum, was ignited by friction. This device was marketed by the 'Repeating Light Co.' of Springfield, Massachusetts. American patents of the nineties made use of a spring-operated lid to fly up and ignite the *amorce* when a catch was pressed.

Some twelve years later, a rather different type of mechanism was popular. This was certainly originated in France. A metal box of specially made circular *amorces* of amadou about half an inch in diameter, each with a hole in the middle and a ring of phosphorus round the hole, was provided with a small compartment at one end. A single *amorce* was put into this compartment, and ignited after the box lid had been closed by turning a knob at one end. An alternative design required a roughened pin to be pulled sharply through a hole in the box, igniting by friction the surrounding ring of phosphorus, and hence the amadou, as it did.

Among the more improbable lighting contrivances, mention should be made of what must have been one of the earliest types of mechanical table lighter produced in about 1870. This was made from bronze in the shape of a Greek lamp. When the two handles at the back were pressed together, a disc inside the body revolved, striking a lump of inflammable material against a rough surface. This burned for five minutes, through the spout of the lamp.

In 1875, lighters were still a novelty, and were very much looked down upon. Fairholt, writing in that year, says, 'Those who are fond of a display of showing materials for obtaining a light, are provided with an elaborate apparatus of silver tubing, through which a smouldering cord of coloured cotton can be drawn, lit by means of a flint, elegantly fashioned from the purest stone, struck against an equally tasteful steel; the whole process being an elegant and costly realization by 'heavy swells' who take tobacco more for the sake of ostentation than pleasure.'

Even as late as 1926, when the first catalogue of the Bryant & May collection of fire-making appliances was published, the author still regarded them as vaguely comic. After saying that they are found mainly in France because of the dearness and badness of French matches, he goes on 'they have been used to a certain extent in Germany also and to a lesser extent in Britain (where they are known popularly as "Lighters"), but for no obvious reason; for in these countries, they offer no advantages over matches, being more troublesome and no cheaper. Indeed, the number of patents covering them which have been taken out in these countries, and the extraordinary variety of the contrivances covered by these patents, suggest a vast amount of wasted ingenuity'. Strong and unprophetic words.

 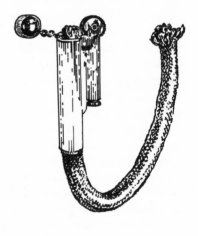

Two early lighters

Lighter in the shape of a book – c. 1920

The most common form of these early lighters was almost identical with the cheapest form of lighter used by millions of French and German countrymen today – a tube containing a long, dangling wick, with a flint and steel device on the top. The 'wick' was not in fact a wick in the proper meaning of the word (a device for sucking up liquid) but a long piece of tinder, impregnated with saltpetre. Nor did the early lighters have a steel wheel to make contact with the flint – the process was little more, as Bryant & May's catalogue said, than an elaborate way of using a flint and steel.

The use of the rare metal cerium, which when compressed with iron filings into a pellet produces an excellent spark against a steel contact, was a considerable advance. So too was the introduction of a spirit lamp at about the turn of the century. Many lighters of this kind were provided with a slip-on cap and a knob and ring projecting from the body. The ring was merely to allow the lighter to be attached to the watch chain. The knob, when pressed, brought together a patch of cerium-and-iron-filings and the inside of the steel cap. When the cap was pulled off sharply, a spark was produced and the wick of the spirit lamp lit. Others, outwardly similar, carried a roll of caps, of the same kind as are used in toy pistols, containing a mildly explosive compound. Pressure on the knob released a striker, which set off the cap and ignited the wick. Another type required a ratchetted plunger at one end to be pulled sharply out.

The introduction of the steel wheel for producing a spark was made in 1909, in Vienna, and the first automatic lighter, which fired when a button in the side was pressed, two years later. The Great War in one way helped to retard the development of the lighter, because the soldiers in the trenches demanded a lighter that would glow, rather than flame and give away their whereabouts to a sniper. Accordingly many thousands of the old tinder cord lighters were made during the four years of the War, well after the improvements of the petrol, wick, and circular steel wheel had been introduced. A large number of lighters of this kind were actually made in the trenches from spent bullet cases.

To bring the story up-to-date, the first butane gas lighter came to England from France in 1950.

6. Matchbox Labels

The collecting of matchbox labels is a specialised business. Devotees have their own society (the British Matchbox Label and Booklet Society) and several magazines. More than one book has been written about the subject.

It should be noted, by the way, that the word *philumenist* (literally 'lover of light'), which was coined to describe a collector of matchbox labels, is never used by serious collectors, who describe themselves simply as 'matchbox label collectors'.

We cannot hope to give a comprehensive account of this offshoot of the world of tobacco bygones, and this chapter is intended only to form an introduction.

The collector recognises five different types of matchbox label. The most common is the *Single Box Label*, a label pasted on top of a sliding tray box. The *All-Round Label*, as its name suggests, is a paper sleeve which wraps round all four sides of the outer cover. The *Skillet* is a cardboard cover which has no separate paper label, but which is printed with the design direct on to the cardboard. The *Pill-box label* is used on the cylindrical match boxes popular in some parts of the world; it is circular and pasted to the top of the lid. The *Banderole* is also used on cylindrical boxes, but is wrapped round the whole container.

We have seen how the match developed from John Walker's invention of the Friction Light in (probably) 1827. They were sold at first in plain cylindrical metal boxes, unlabelled. The first label in the world was also an English product, and appeared in 1829. The box it adorned contained Samuel Jones' Lucifers, and the label (a 'single box label') carried without any other embellishments the printed words 'S. Jones's Lucifer Matches, that ignite by the friction produced by drawing the match briskly through a piece of sandpaper and are warranted never to impair by keeping. Inventor of the Prometheans, Self-Acting Coffee Pot, Etnas, etc. Light-house, 201 Strand, London.'

Early Lucifer matchbox

Walker first label, which came out after Jones', was similar, and read –

> *Walker's Friction Matches. 100 Matches. Price One Shilling. As used in the household of His Majesty King William IV. John Walker, Stockton-on-Tees.*

These two are, of course, the most desirable labels in the world to the collector.

The pictorial label which we know today was preceded in England and elsewhere by labels which carried a description of the contents, often in flowery terms and with a wealth of scroll-work, but no pictures. The first known pictorial label appeared in 1830. It was

Later Lucifer box

brown and green, and showed an Englishman and a Scot smoking. It was stuck to a box of 'Royal Patent Lucifers' by the makers, N. Jones & Co. A pictorial label was also produced in America in the same year.

English matchbox labels, in the same way as the cigarette cards of later years, cut a representative section through the social history of the country in the nineteenth and, to some extent, the twentieth century. Most of the royal landmarks were recorded – the marriage of Queen Victoria and Albert in 1840, of the Prince of Wales and Princess Alexandra in 1863, the Golden Jubilee in 1887. Notable public figures were commemorated, among them Arthur Orton, the Tichborne claimant in 1867; Sir Robert Lowe, a politician who might not have been sufficiently famous to be pictured on a matchbox label had he not proposed a tax on matches in 1871; and many others. Among events which were recorded in this way were the 1851 Great Exhibition and the introduction of the Victoria Cross in 1857. Even the Manchester Exhibition of 1887 was not forgotten.

Social injustices were pilloried by means of this widespread and cheap form of advertising. One of the pioneers in this form of attack was the Salvation Army match factory, which was opened in 1891 and operated for nine years. At this time the workers in the match industry were paid appallingly low wages, and many suffered from the occupational scourge, 'Phossy Jaw', caused by the dangerous yellow phosphorus used in the match heads. The Salvation Army's factory at Old Ford in London was opened to give workers better pay and conditions, and it trumpeted its cause on the box labels. The matches were called 'Lights in Darkest England', and the labels carried slogans such as 'To fight against sweating', or 'To raise the wages of the matchbox makers'.

Similar in its intentions was a later factory, the 'Dunyerbit' Safety Match factory which for a few years from 1922 employed disabled soldiers of the Great War, and issued its boxes with red, white and blue labels.

Charity labels, where a small extra amount is charged for the box and given to the charity advertised, have never been popular in this country, and it has been left to others to use them. Holland was the first to do so in 1928 during the world-wide depression of those years.

The Scandinavian countries have issued many charity labels, and continue to do so at intervals.

Sweden, the world's leading match-producer, began to build up her enormous export trade as early as 1848. In 1854 Sweden produced her first 'sulphur safety matches', the label of which announced 'Patent Safety-Matches (without Phosphorus) Important Discovery': this label was the first to be printed on the now-familiar yellow paper.

That forgeries occur even in the unexpected field of matchbox label collecting is shown by the known two hundred and fifty-odd imitations of the original Swedish match factory's label (known to collectors as the 'Jönköpings original'), printed in black and yellow in the eighteen forties and showing medallions on each side saying 'Safety Matches' and 'Strike only on the box'.

One Swedish speciality has been the production to order of personal matchbox labels. Many notable figures throughout the world have had their own labels printed in this way, including King Farouk (the arms of Egypt on a beige background) 'Pandit Nehru (red and white, including his initials)' Eva Peron (her photograph) and many others. That labels do not have to be particularly old, or even particularly rare, for them to be valued by collectors is shown by a set of national costume labels first issued in Sweden in 1935. Twelve designs with a background of purple were issued; the high standard of the art work and the excellent colouring have made this set eagerly sought-after.

A unique type of box was produced by the Swedish match industry early in the present century. This was basically the familiar sliding-tray box, but instead of one tray there were two, one above the other. The intention was that the second (empty) tray should be a rubbish bin for used matches, but the idea never became popular. This large box had an all-round label, and is a considerable rarity.

The Norwegian match industry was founded in 1840, and from the early days Norwegian matches were exported to England. Some of the most eagerly-collected labels are those known to collectors as 'Norwegian Sulphurs'. They were issued between 1874 and 1888 in considerable quantity for the English (or rather the English-speaking) market for boxes of sulphur matches, and are printed in red on white. This colour scheme was traditional for sulphur matches, and was followed in other countries which produced them – notably Sweden, India and Japan. Many of the 'Norwegian Sulphurs' were printed for the Indian market with such labels as 'The Great Mogul', 'The Rupee' and the 'Snake Charmer'. Two for the English market, now of considerable scarcity, are 'London Bridge' (1882) and 'The British Colonies' (1888). But probably the most celebrated of all Norwegian labels is the 'Red Cross' issued in 1883 on a box of sulphur matches. It had to be withdrawn in 1915 as a result of the international agreement that the Red Cross should not be used for advertisement purposes, and was superseded by the 'Blue Cross' label still used. Although it was issued for 32 years, very few specimens have survived. Other 'Red Cross' labels were issued in Glasgow (this was actually the first, and is even rarer than the Norwegian label), Belgium, Sweden and India. Among the many public-spirited labels which have been issued in Norway is one example printed in 1945 which announced in Norwegian 'He who drinks Methanol (wood-alcohol) is blind and becomes blind'.

Denmark produced in 1837 what is now one of the rarest labels, that of the Copenhagen factory of Rohmel and Schüere. Some of the most modern of Danish issues are also well thought of among collectors for their high standard of production. An excellent set of twelve labels printed in black, blue and mauve, showing Danish Industries and Sports and issued as recently as 1958, is already scarce.

Among the most interesting Danish labels are two which were secretly printed in black on mauve paper (a traditional Danish combination of colours in matchbox label printing) during the last war, while Denmark was under German occupation. One of these imitated a well-known design of the Hellerup factory showing King Christian X, but substituted a portrait of Stalin for the King. Instead of the normal wording round the frame describing the matches and giving the name of the factory, however, there appeared –

The Victory of the Soviet Union is our Freedom.

Use these, sabotage German work. Long Live a free Denmark.

The other resistance label showed a burning swastika, with the words 'Fight for a Free Denmark'.

Finland was once the main exporter of matches to Britain, the

U.S.A. and Australia, and very many labels of high quality have come out of that country. The earliest labels were printed in both Russian and Finnish, most of the original factories having been set up by Russians. Among later labels of interest are the 'Char-a-Banc Safety Matches' showing one of those almost forgotten open buses of the twenties; and sets of twelve scenes from various parts of Finland, first issued in 1939 and again from 1950, each label made from a woodcut.

The best-known rare Finnish label is the 'Central Sentry'. A red and green label, printed on yellow, normally showed a sentry in his box on the left-hand side of the label. For a very short period, however, the design was changed to show the sentry in the middle of the label.

The United States was quickly off the mark with its match industry, for wax vestas were being made in the early eighteen thirties, and 'friction lights' soon afterwards. Some of the earliest American labels are particularly interesting because of the Revenue Act of 1862, which added a tax to the sale of matches (according to the contents of the box) and required the makers to produce their own stamps to show that it had been paid. Many of the match manufacturers incorporated the stamp into the design of the label. The tax remained in force until 1883. A nice piece of advertising was seen in one of these early label-cum-tax-stamp issues of about 1877:

> These matches have been sold for FORTY YEARS, and have WITHSTOOD THE DAMP and HUMID atmosphere of EVERY CLIMATE when all others have failed. Shippers and Sea Captains invariably give OUR MATCHES THE PREFERENCE.

This was printed on the side panel of the label. The front panel was printed in black and white with portraits of the founders, Messrs Byam and Carlton.

A patriotic label issued in 1915 (copied from an early English label of the same type) was issued to the troops in France, and boasted punningly 'A Match for the World'. This was a 'skillet' label and showed the British and American flags. A large number of patriotic labels of different kinds were also issued during the Second World War.

The earliest American label (and one which goes against the general run of events by being a pictorial label) was issued in 1830, the same year as Jones' first label in England. It was produced by a firm in Troy

(New York) and read 'Sulphur matches manufactured by V. R. Powell, Troy, N. Y.', with a picture of a horse-drawn trap.

After a slow start, the American match labels grew in volume until there is now a colossal number of labels (mostly skillets) of varying quality. Some are excellently produced. America more than any other country has used the skillet as a vehicle for advertising.

Mexico has produced some of the finest labels in the world, although the standard has declined somewhat since about 1930. Most labels are all-round ones or skillets. Here, as in many other countries, a tax is paid on each box, evidenced by a stamp which seals the end. Popular in Mexico are the 'spring-flap' type of boxes, in which a cardboard cover is automatically raised by a piece of elastic when the tray is pushed out. One might suspect that the manufacturers manipulate the collectors' market with some skill; enormously long sets are issued, a few at a time, or particular labels in a set are sold for only a short period.

Russia started making matches in 1837, but the earliest labels preserved date from about 1880. Pre-revolutionary labels are on the whole dull, non-pictorial, and all very similar, because of a virtual monopoly in the match-making industry. Some portraits of the Czars and the Imperial coat-of-arms were also produced, however.

After the Revolution of 1917, labels took on a fiercely patriotic note. Between the two wars a large number of extremely crudely-printed labels of this type were issued, many of them quite obviously on salvaged waste paper. In the Second World War, encouraging slogans were printed on matchboxes issued to the troops, as had been done in Western Europe and America in the Great War. Today, Russia rivals America in her output of up-to-date designs.

Austria specialised in oblong labels designed for cylindrical boxes (in sets of three, usually showing country or domestic scenes), and in banderole labels. From 1900 until the start of the Great War, some labels were issued showing European royalty whose thrones have now disappeared for ever. Before the start of the present century, many sulphur-match labels printed in the traditional red were produced. During the Second World War, two historic labels were printed in Austria – one with the Nazi slogan 'Ein Reich, Ein Volk, Ein Führer' and the other a 'Camel' label in brown and fawn for issue to Rommel's *Afrika Korps.*

The earliest (about 1833) German matches were sold in plain paper wrappers, but within two years labels were commonly used. One label issued in 1835 by the Kammerer factory was attached to a box of Congreve matches intended for export to England, and packed for greater safety in bran inside the box. The white label showed a picture of the matches, and carried the following instructions. *These matches, invented and improved by Congreve, must, as the above drawing shews, be taken between two fingers, and the box, being previously shut again, thei may be instantly lighted by softly rubbing them against the bottom of the box itself, although the same effect is produced by softly rubbing them against ani other hard substance – J. C. K.*
Not bad for 1835; we see worse effects today under similar circumstances.

From 1911 onwards, German labels for the home market were marked with a factory number in the top left-hand corner. The same system, using letters in the bottom right hand corner, is current in France.

In France, matches under the name of *Alumettes Infernales*, were being produced in 1832. They were held in a cardboard box with a slip-on lid bearing detailed instructions. In 1845, Le Verrier's cigar-tips were on sale in similar boxes with a black-and-white label of instructions stuck on the top. French matches, whether this is justified or not, have an international reputation for unreliability.

Japan started producing her own matches in 1875. By 1881 she was exporting them, and by 1912 she was one of the three main match producers of the world. An enormous variety of labels was issued, many of the earlier ones being imitations of European labels in the dishonourable pre-war way that Japan had (one hastens to say that Japan has no need to imitate anyone now). Two classes are worthy of special mention. During the 1920's in particular, some wonderful instructions and slogans were printed on boxes destined for the English-speaking market – such things as 'Made in (Rectitude kindly) Japan' and 'Watertight Matches' and 'Guaranteed the not damps'. The other class is of propaganda labels issued during the last war.

Over thirty designs in bright colours, showing caricatures of Allied leaders, or pictures of Japanese armed might, were made.

Italy has produced some of the finest labels of all. Indeed, the collecting of labels became a national passion in Italy during the eighteen eighties until it was overtaken by the equally passionate collection of postcards. Matches were produced from 1831, but the original containers were merely brown paper cartons. One factory later produced a set of brown and white banderole-type labels of European royalty, similar to those made in Austria (see above). From about 1870 some magnificient labels produced by chromo-lithography were issued as 'skillets'. Subjects varied widely, but nearly all were extremely artistic. These excellent labels were made until 1896, when a Manufacturing Tax was imposed which made the enterprise a financial impossibility.

The Australian match-making industry was started in 1871 at Melbourne. The earliest labels were distinguished by the coat-of-arms of Victoria in red on yellow paper. The early Australian matches were rather different from any others for they were produced in blocks divided into individual matches almost completely, but leaving the ends joined together – in the same way as modern card-board book matches are joined at the other end. The earliest label had 'Colonial Block Matches' as its title. In 1896 the 'pillbox' label was introduced. This was stuck on one end of a round box, matched at the other end by the striking surface. This shape rapidly became popular, and remained so until 1950. Miners in the goldfields found the boxes handy for holding sovereigns.

India has produced a colossal output of labels ranging from the most crudely-printed affairs to examples of high quality. Subjects are very varied, but religious themes, Hindu mythology, patriotic and (later) independence slogans and Congress symbols are all characteristic.

Certain details in a label help the collector to identify the country of origin of the label itself (for all the large-scale match-producing countries have carried on a wide export trade, and have printed labels for their customers). For example, a crossbow device in one corner means that the label was printed in Switzerland, and an inverted mushroom indicates Israel. The French state monopoly contracted with many countries to supply matches (including labelled boxes) from 1935 onwards, and the production country was identified by a letter in one corner. These letters range from A (Russia) to UA (Belgium). This is only one example of the semi-secret coding of labels. The serious collector is advised to consult a specialist work such as *Collecting Matchbox Labels* by Joan Rendell.

7. Snuff

Reports of snuff (which in its basic form is nothing more than powdered tobacco) were brought back from Columbus' second voyage to the Americas in 1494; and one of the very earliest of tobacco bygones was the cane tube, about a foot long, which the natives used to sniff up the grains.

Ireland took to snuff long before England did. By the middle of the seventeenth century the Irish were as heavy snuffers as the English were pipe-smokers. Simple wooden boxes were carried by all classes, and the snuff (known to its users as 'Smutchin') was sniffed up through a quill in exactly the same way as Columbus' Indians had used a cane two hundred years earlier.

Although snuff-taking did not become popular throughout England until the eighteenth century, it was certainly practised here in the preceding era, largely by undergraduates (who, as always, were anxious to set new fashions) and by travellers who came under the influence of the French. One reason for its spread was that the habit of smoking was by this time so firmly entrenched, in even the very lowest classes, that 'Society', and particularly its younger members, felt that it was time to adopt a less common habit. By about 1700, smoking and snuffing were almost equally popular.

Snuff of a kind was used as early as 1614, when in the plague of that year it was found to be useful as a sort of explosive antiseptic. By the time of the more famous plague of 1665 it was a recognised form of protection against the disease, and was increasingly being used for the pleasures it gave. It was from this period that walking sticks began to be made with a receptacle for snuff under the head, so that a gentleman could extract a pinch as he strolled along.

It was however almost the end of the century before snuff could be bought ready ground, fine or coarse, plain or flavoured and scented to appeal to every individual nose. The seventeenth century snuffer bought his snuff in a partially-manufactured state, in the form of a solid roll of hard tobacco a few inches long, descriptively called a *Carotte*. When he wanted to produce some snuff, the carotte was rubbed against a grater and the powder collected into a box.

Pocket Snuff-Rasps

Pocket snuff-rasps were made in great variety to keep pace with the rising graph of snuff-consumption from the mid-seventeenth century onwards. Early examples are crude and functional, consisting of no more than an oblong sheet of metal in a wooden frame, some three or four inches long and perforated with crudely punched holes in the

Pocket snuff rasp set in a shell

manner of a modern cheese-grater. The end of the carotte was rubbed over the holes and the resultant powder fell into the box below. An opening in the end of the box allowed the snuff to be extracted. The fineness of the snuff, which later became as much a matter of individual choice as the flavour, depended upon the size of the punched holes. Some snuff boxes of this period, particularly those made in the cheaper materials such as horn, incorporated a roughened surface on one side which acted as a makeshift grater.

As snuff became more widely popular with the advent of the eighteenth century, snuff rasps became more elaborate and were made from finer materials. A cover for the perforated grill was incorporated. This was of wood or ivory, often finely carved or decorated with gold and silver piqué work. The cover is usually mounted on a pin at one end of the box so that it can be swung aside to reveal the grater. Many

Snuff rasp with ivory cover

of the most elaborate rasps were of French origin; some excellent examples may be seen in the Pinto Collection of Wooden Bygones, recently acquired by Birmingham.

In the early, unpretentious English snuff-rasps, the rasp was made of iron; more elaborate rasps were of blue steel, or occasionally of brass. Many of the early eighteenth century rasps were fitted with a separate compartment for holding the newly-ground snuff as well as the carotte of tobacco. Some of the more elaborate examples were provided with a large container at one end, in which a day's supply of grated snuff was carried; and a much smaller one at the other, into which a single (though generous) pinch of freshly-grated snuff could be separately shaken.

Some outsize rasps of plain workmanship may be found, measuring up to two feet in length. These were used by shops and coffee houses

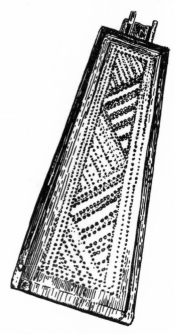

Snuff rasp for shop use

for the preparation of wholesale quantities.

A snuff-rasp of quite different type consists of two eggcup-shaped containers mounted one on top of the other; a perforated grill divides the two. It was probably used in a shop or inn. Somewhat similar is the early Scottish snuff-mill. This was a personal piece of equipment, made up of two wooden parts: a little barrel-shaped container, and a lid fitted with a projection on its underside which went down to the bottom of the container. The end of the projection was studded with rough metal points, and ground pieces of tobacco leaf to powder when the handle was turned. Some later Scottish snuff boxes were made in a very similar form, but without the projection on the underside of the lid. This mid-eighteenth century design was purely a container for ready-ground snuff.

Snuff in wholesale quantities was also prepared in small mortars of hard wood. It is virtually impossible to distinguish snuff-makers' mortars from those used by apothecaries for preparing drugs, but the pestle, which did the grinding in the mortar, was of a peculiar shape. It was a hard wooden ball mounted on a handle, and at the opposite side to the handle was a further projection about two inches long, rather like the rudiments of another handle. This projection was used for stirring in the scents and spices which fashionable society was demanding should be mixed with its snuff in ever-increasing variety.

The death-knell of the individual pocket snuff rasp was sounded by Admiral Sir George Rooke in 1702. His fleet captured near Cadiz a number of Spanish ships which contained, among other desirable spoils, hundreds of casks filled with fine Spanish snuff; and later on during the same voyage he seized quantities of the best Havana snuff at Vigo. All this was sold off at knock-down prices (fourpence a pound on average) in the sea-ports when Rooke's fleet returned. It was hardly surprising that the flood of cheap, high-grade snuff found eager takers. Very largely because of this episode, snuffers of all classes were soon demanding ready-made snuff in ever-increasing varieties, and elegant containers to keep it in; few people were prepared to follow the habits of either Frederick the Great or Dr. Johnson, both of whom kept large quantities of snuff loose in their pockets, to the detriment of their clothes.

Snuff-Boxes

It would take a complete book to describe adequately the enormous number of snuff-boxes produced in the eighteenth century. They were made from every possible material, and in an endless variety of shapes. It is often difficult to distinguish them from the other small boxes (for such things as comfits, patches or rouge) which were also carried by both sexes during the same period.

Certainly the most famous of snuff-boxes are the wonderful pieces of craftsmanship in precious materials produced in France from the time of Louis XIII until the end of the eighteenth century. They can hardly be regarded as true snuff-boxes, for few of them were actually used as such. The most gorgeous (there is no other word for them) of the French snuff-boxes of this type were made during the reigns of Louis XV and XVI, a period of the greatest magnificence at the French court. Gold boxes, heavily encrusted with diamonds, or set with miniatures after Fragonard or Boucher in enamels were given as tokens of favours (usually political) – favours both received and expected.

Gold snuff box

Such masterpieces of the jewellers' art fetch as much as £10,000 on the occasions when they appear in the market today.

Gold and silver English snuff-boxes of the same period are less ornate and generally rely for their decorative appeal on engraving and embossing of the metal, rather than inset jewels or enamelled scenes and portraits. Even among these superb creations, a distinction is drawn between table snuff-boxes and those intended to be carried in the pocket. Size is not always a guide, because the Georgian coat pocket was a much more capacious receptacle than its modern equivalent; table boxes were usually made with a lid which could be removed, whereas a pocket snuff-box was fitted with a hinged lid, designed not only to prevent the lid from coming off in the pocket, but also to make as tight a seal as possible against the fine grains of snuff finding their way into the pocket.

This was an ever-present problem, and it was not properly solved for the general snuff-taking public until the invention of the Laurencekirk box (see below). Many of the table boxes were closed by detachable lids fixed in position by a half-turn against a threaded groove. This was also effective in keeping away the air, for snuff is temperamental and soon loses its flavour and consistency if it is allowed to dry out. Such a thing was not to be allowed after a Georgian gentleman (or lady) had taken infinite pains to choose just the snuff which suited his nose and his personality.

The variety available by the middle of the eighteenth century was prodigious, as the records of Messrs Fribourg & Treyer – still firmly established at their original shop in the Haymarket – show. All snuff of any pretensions to quality was imported, and the names given to the blends have an exotic ring – Brazil, Cabinet Havannah, Curaçoa, Dutch Bran, Domingo, Étrennes (very popular with Beau Brummel, this one), French Carotte, High Toast (an Irish snuff, deliberately over-dried), Martinique, Masulipatam, Morocco, Oronoko, Rapé de Lyons, Scholten, Spanish Sabilla, Tongear, Violet Strasbourg – these are only a few. As a matter of interest, this same firm today still offers as many as forty-three varieties. Not included among them is a snuff which was very popular in Italy – Odeur de Rome.

Ivory and *tortoiseshell* were other materials used for high quality snuff-boxes in the eighteenth century. They were popular presents, particularly in Court and government circles. In 1820, when snuffing was in decline, part of the Coronation expenses of

Wooden (top) and tortoiseshell snuff boxes

George IV was for snuff boxes presented to foreign ministers. The amount was over eight thousand pounds. Tortoiseshell in particular had the advantage of maintaining snuff in good condition, for its insulating properties meant that the snuff remained at an even temperature. Many tortoiseshell boxes were decorated with piqué work in gold and silver, initially in France where this method of decoration was developed, but also in England. Ivory boxes were also embellished with piqué work during the same period.

An enormous number of *silver* snuff-containers were made, some of basic shape and with a minimum of decoration, others finely wrought and chased, or set with gold and other precious materials. The English have always had a particular affection for the plain beauty of silver, and this taste is reflected in the quantity and variety of silver boxes made for snuff-addicts of all but those with the lowest level of income. Among the infinite range of designs, mention should be made of the silver-mounted cowrie-shell which was extremely popular for about two decades at the end of the seventeenth century.

Silver snuff-boxes are often lined internally with a thin layer of gilding. Gold does not tarnish, and the lining prevents the snuff from taking up the silver oxide which would be produced by exposure to the air.

Silver table-boxes were used in most large houses for the ceremonial round of after-dinner snuff. Most were plain but often engraved with the owner's crest or initials. Some were more elaborate, as for example the table snuff container which consisted of a winged cupid pushing a wheelbarrow in which the snuff was found, the whole piece mounted on four wheels so that it could be passed easily from guest to guest.

Enamelled metal boxes were popular in the mid-eighteenth century. Although some of the finer examples came from the famous establishments at Battersea and Bilston, there were a large number of potteries in Staffordshire producing enamelled snuff and other boxes; many of them were of very indifferent quality. As well as the basic square and oblong shapes, novelties in enamelled ware were popular, and included such things as miniature pianos and other musical instruments.

Some *porcelain* snuff-boxes were made, almost entirely on the Continent (Meissen specialised in them for a while during the 1730's). They must be regarded more as novelties than as snuff-containers because of their fragility. They were certainly never intended to be carried about in the pocket. However, they were meticulously made,

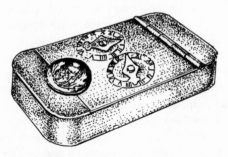

Snuff box with combination lock

as one might expect from the Meissen factory; and particular attention was paid to the silver mountings which formed the lid. Some pretty designs were used – a hen with a clutch of chickens, or a Watteau-type shepherdess. Porcelain was also used in the form of painted panels mounted on expensive boxes in precious metals.

Wooden snuff-boxes were made in such profusion that it would be impossible to give a comprehensive list of the designs, even if space allowed. Every type of wood was used, often in combinations, and the range of shapes runs from the plain, unadorned miniature chest to fancies of such extravagance that it is often difficult to decide if the result is a snuff box, or indeed a box at all. All the devices of trick openings, secret containers, dual purpose boxes and other attractions have been incorporated. Perhaps the most entertaining of these – remarkable too for the light it throws on the hold which snuff-taking had on the whole population at the time – are the two or three examples in this country of secret snuff-containers, hidden by a sliding panel, hollowed out in the end of a church pew. There is one of these in the choir stalls of the parish church at Middleton in Lancashire.

It was a favourite occupation among apprentices of all kinds during the eighteenth century to make snuff-boxes in shapes connected with their own trades – shoes by shoemakers, smoothing-planes by carpenters, hats by hatters, barrels by coopers, coffins, boats, and so on. There were also many so-called snuff-boxes made in wood to completely fanciful shapes – coiled snakes and nightmare faces and figures – and a considerable number carved from famous trees or timbers. Shakespeare's mulberry at Stratford produced more snuff-boxes than one would have thought possible, as did both Robin Hood's and King Charles' oak trees. Many old warships were turned into snuff-boxes and other novelties. It should be said that this outbreak of historic cannibalism was very largely a late nineteenth century disease, and a tourist trap.

The shoe-shape was extremely popular, and became a widely bought attraction in the late eighteenth and nineteenth centuries. As a rule, the top of the shoe was fashioned into a sliding lid, and very often the sole and heel were studded with minute brass nails. Many of these boxes were made more for their appearance than their utility as snuff-containers, and the lids are frequently of little use in separating the snuff inside from the air. This was a defect which was by no means confined to such crudely-made wooden boxes. In all but the most precisely made (and therefore expensive) examples, the weak point of the box in this respect was its hinge. It was not until the end of the eighteenth century that the problem was solved; the solution provides one of the most engaging chapters in the story of snuff.

Popular victorian snuff boxes

The Laurencekirk box was the invention of James Sandy, a cripple living at Laurencekirk in Kincardineshire. He had lost the use of his legs entirely as a child, and was permanently bed-ridden. Far from allowing this to cripple his extremely active brain as well, however, he turned his bed into a fully-equipped workshop. He designed the bed himself and had it made in the village. It was circular and fitted with platforms and shelves on which he fixed lathes, vices, cases of tools, and everything else he needed to work not only in wood, but in metal and glass as well. Sandy seems to have been an extremely likeable man as well as a character in his own right, and his strange workshop-bed became the focal point of the village. Nothing in the way of fine work appears to have been beyond his capabilities and resources; he made clocks, musical instruments of high quality, optically accurate telescopes, and an impressive selection of fine furniture. One of his amiable eccentricities was to hatch out under his bedclothes wild birds' eggs brought by his visitors, until his room was filled with his foster-chicks.

Sandy spent altogether nearly fifty years in his bed, applying his mind and his talents to problems of craftsmanship. The hinge which was his most lasting contribution consists, in its most usual form, of seven rollers, alternately cut in one with the lid and the body of the box, and then fitted together and joined by a brass pin running down the centre of all the rollers. The great merit of this hinge was that it was all part of the box itself and required no foreign materials to be fixed to the wood, causing problems of gaps and uneven wear. The hinge required the most accurate of workmanship however, for the tiny rollers had to meet exactly to prevent fine snuff grains from working their way between them. This was Sandy's triumph, for his hinges – made with special tools which he himself designed for the purpose – met together with engineering precision. The other main feature of the Laurencekirk snuff-boxes was the internal flange of the lid, which fitted into the box when it was closed, to provide a close-fitting seal that was very nearly airtight. This was carved in one with the lid. The Laurencekirk boxes, as they soon came to be called, very rapidly became popular throughout Scotland and indeed the making of them was a major industry in the country within a few years. The wood used was usually plane.

Decorations applied to the finished boxes varied considerably. Two of the most familiar types are the black transfer prints of places of

Wooden snuff box showing Laurencekirk hinge

national or local interest, applied to the plain wood of a finished box
lid and then varnished over; and the various tartan patterns, known
generally as *Mauchlin ware* from the centre of activity of the firm which
made most of them. Both these popular types of decoration were
extensively used on other surfaces than snuff-box lids, of course; and
the manufacture of both was not slow in moving across the border
into England as soon as it was realised how profitable the trade in
them was proving.

The main defect in the Laurencekirk box from the snuff-taker's
point of view was that the thin plane wood was not at all successful in
keeping the snuff inside in the slightly moist state that most users
preferred. Accordingly all boxes of this type were lined with a layer of
tin foil. It is rare today to find a nineteenth century Laurencekirk box
with its foil intact, but traces almost invariably remain. Another
disadvantage of these boxes which became apparent as time went by
was the extreme delicacy of the hinge. It needed only one rough
opening of the lid for the hinge to snap. The century and a half that
have gone by since Laurencekirk boxes appeared in quantity has taken
a heavy toll of the meticulously-made hinges, as collectors have found.

The drawback of wooden snuff-boxes in allowing the contents to
become dry and dusty, even when the boxes were lined, was serious
enough for the regular snuffer to allow wood to be almost completely
ousted by *papier mâché* shortly after this new material made its
appearance at the end of the eighteenth century. In spite of its French
name, it was an English development of an ancient Persian invention,
and was originally known here as 'Paper mash' or 'Paper ware'. Its
great merit for the making of snuff-boxes was its insulating properties
against heat, cold, air and damp; it was also cheap to produce. The
smooth surface lent itself very well to decoration, and a large proportion of the many thousands of papiermâché snuff-boxes that were
produced in the nineteenth century is embellished with paintings in
oils. The subjects are too numerous to list. Another popular method
of decorating papiermâché was with inset mother-of-pearl (this was
by no means confined to snuff-boxes; papiermâché with mother-of-
pearl inlay was used for a wide range of decorative and useful objects,
even to the extent of full-sized furniture). One particularly valued

type of papiermâché for snuff-boxes was made from potato skins.

Horn was a popular material for cheap snuff-boxes from the earliest days of snuff-taking. The Scottish horn boxes and mulls are mentioned below. These relatively unimproved horns were also widely used in country districts of England. More elaborate were the eighteenth century boxes made from animal hooves, often beautifully finished and polished, and usually fitted with a silver lid. Horn could also be steamed and pressed into shape in the same way as tortoise-shell, and a large number of circular boxes of this kind were made, usually with a moulded design impressed into the lid; hunting scenes are very common.

Snuff-mulls

Scotland has always had a close connection with snuff. It was fashion-able there some considerable time before it ousted smoking in England, largely because of the sympathy that existed between the Scots and the French in the seventeenth century. Much later the Laurencekirk box, too, added to the fame of Scotland in matters connected with snuff. In the early days of Scottish snuffing however, by far the most common receptacle for snuff, both for home use and for carrying about in the pocket, was a length of natural horn fitted with a stopper of some kind. The embellishments fixed to the horn, and the means of stoppering it, varied widely according to the financial resources of the owner. Crofters sealed the open end with a plug of wood, and the horn itself was probably a piece from one of their own mountain rams. The fashionable Scottish snuff-taker used a horn decorated with engraved silver, and with the hinged lid perhaps set with a jewel; the native cairngorm was popular for this purpose. These Scottish snuff containers were known as 'mulls', a word which is a dialect variant of 'mills'. It stems from the days when they had to grind their own snuff from the coarse *Carotte* of tobacco, and to do it carried about with them the miniature graters already described.

An ingenious variety of horn mull gives out a single pinch of snuff from the pointed end of the horn when a knob is turned. The pinch falls into a miniature cup provided for the purpose. Like the Chinese snuff-bottles (which are described below), some snuff-mulls

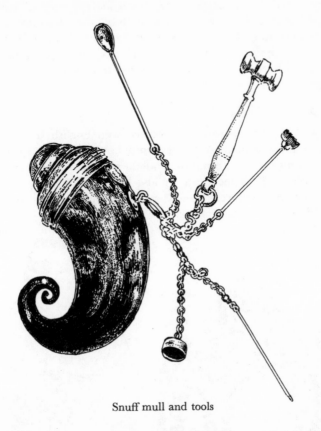

Snuff mull and tools

were provided with a snuffing spoon, but this has rarely survived.

The pinnacle of the snuff mull's magnificence is seen in the table examples made, mostly during the eighteenth and early nineteenth centuries, for the messes of Scottish regiments. Single and double horns, often marvellously curled, were mounted on a base of wood or silver and usually embellished with a considerable amount of silver. The snuff container was set in the end of a single horn, and capped with silver, or between double horns as a separate silver box. The most spectacular of these table mulls have compartments for several different types of snuff, and a range of miniature instruments in silver attached by chains to the base – a hare's foot to wipe the upper lip, a spoon (or 'nose shovel' as it was usually called), a rake to smooth the surface before taking a pinch; a brush to sweep away spilt grains and even a tiny hammer to loosen caked snuff from the sides of the mull.

Chinese Snuff Bottles

Although we are primarily concerned with English snuff-taking, mention must be made of Chinese snuff bottles, if only because they are certainly the most beautiful of all the collectors' items concerned with tobacco. Their inclusion can also be justified in the knowledge that many were imported from China in an unfinished state, and fitted with silver caps in this country.

Chinese snuff bottles

Snuff bottles were carried in the sleeve, and range in size from about two to six inches in height. They have narrow necks and a tightly-fitting stopper, to the end of which is attached a long spoon which reaches to the bottom of the bottle. The word 'bottle' indicates glass, but although many snuff bottles were indeed made of glass, a wide range of other materials was also used in making them. Ivory, porcelain, precious and semi-precious stone (such as jade and agate), red lacquer and enamels were all used. The finer examples are miracles of decoration, particular attention being paid to making use of natural effects in the material. Certainly the most interesting type of decoration was the painting of the inside surface of glass bottles; how this was done through the narrow neck is still a mystery, but the most likely explanation is simply a combination of a fine brush, incredible delicacy of touch, and endless patience.

Snuff bottles may have been made in China at the latter end of the seventeenth century, but most were produced in the eighteenth and early nineteenth centuries, exactly the same period as the fashionable English were also occupied with snuff to the exclusion of all other forms of tobacco enjoyment.

One relic of snuffing which the collector will *not* find is the *snuff pistol*, which a satirical non-snuffing gentleman writing in the London Journal 'invented' in the early years of Victoria's reign. This double-barrelled instrument was to be applied to the nose and, when the triggers were pulled, would deliver enough snuff to last the whole day.

8. Trade Signs, Tokens and Cards

Among the few larger items connected with tobacco that the collector may come across are the tobacconist's and snuff-seller's trade-signs. The word tobacconist is here used in its modern sense of a tobacco seller. In the seventeenth century it meant a smoker of tobacco. Until Acts of Parliament in the seventeen sixties prohibited them, every shopkeeper had a sign board, or a representation of the goods he sold, hung above his shop. They were not just for decoration. Addison, writing in the *Spectator* in 1711, had said 'I would enjoin every shop to make use of a sign which bears some affinity to the wares in which he deals'. Few of the people could read, and these simple representations – the cobbler's boot, the sweep's brush, or the grocer's three gilded sugar-loaves – advertised the wares inside the premises as no lettering could have done. The trouble was that the signs got larger and heavier as the years went by, and the fixing less and less secure, until these overhanging structures of iron and wood had become a very real danger to the people who walked under them. When the laws abolished them, the tobacco trade was less affected than most others, because apart from one type of sign most of the traditional tobacco and snuff-sellers' trade emblems were carved figures that stood at the shop entrance. The exception was the *Tobacco Roll* (also called, with the abandoned spelling of contemporary records, Tobacco Rowle and Tobacco Role). A few examples still survive in their original places – there is one in Dover and one in Worcester at least – over the door of a tobacconist. To the modern eye they are meaningless, but in the eighteenth century they were the most familiar of all tobacconists signs. The sign represents a

Tobacco roll trade sign

bale of 'twist', which was made out of a long rope of spun tobacco leaves, coiled into the shape of a drum for ease of handling. In the sign, which was carved from wood, the twists are usually painted black and gold alternately. The sign is known to have been in use in London in the year of the Great Fire, 1666.

The tobacco roll sign is linked with the next, one of the most attractive of all trade signs and one which even today has not lost its meaning. David Wishart, who kept a tobacco and snuff shop in Coventry Street, London, originated the *Highlander Figure*. His trade-card in 1720 showed a Highlander in trews, not the kilt, a flat hat and carrying a sword and shield on his arm. In the background lay a tobacco roll. Wishart's shop, *At ye Highlander, Thistle and Crown* to give it its full title, sold Scottish snuff as a speciality – 'High and

Highlander figure,
a snuff seller's
trade sign

low dry'd Scots snuff' as he said. It also appears that it became a
meeting place for Jacobite sympathisers after the abortive rebellion of
1715. In about 1720, Wishart had made a figure similar to the one in
his trade card. There was no obvious connection with tobacco or snuff,
other than the Scots snuff which he sold; and to the Jacobites it was
a rallying point and a sign of defiance.

After the second Jacobite rising in 1745, George II became
somewhat sensitive on the subject of the Scots, and the wearing of
Highland dress was prohibited under severe penalties in 1747. An
amusing paragraph appeared in a newspaper soon after:

*We hear that the dapper wooden Highlanders, who guard so heroically the
doors of snuff-shops, intend to petition the Legislature, in order that they
may be excused from complying with the Act of Parliament with regard to
their change of dress; alledging that they have ever been faithfull subjects
of his Majesty, having constantly supplied his Guards with a pinch out of
their Mulls when they marched by them, and so far from engaging in any
Rebellion, that they have never entertained a rebellious thought; whence
they humbly hope that they shall not be put to the expense of buying new cloaths.*

It is clear from this piece that Wishart's fancy had been copied
extensively in London, and perhaps elsewhere, by this time. The law
banning Highland dress was eventually repealed in the seventeen
eighties, and the life-sized carved wooden figure, now wearing the kilt
and a Highland bonnet and holding a snuff mull or box in one hand,
was soon the universal sign for a snuff trader – particularly in Scotland
itself, which is perhaps surprising: national dress is not much used for
advertisement purposes in its own country. Equally surprising is that
practically all the carved and painted Highland figures used in
Scotland were made in England. There are several Highlander signs to
be seen in this country, some still used for their original purpose
(examples are in Cheltenham, in London, in Dover and in Ipswich).
Most are life-sized, but they vary from about seven feet to two
feet in height. The London Museum in Kensington Palace has a
collection of five. They seem to have gone out of regular use as a
trade sign in about 1845, and from that date onwards they began to
be regarded as curiosities.

Probably the oldest of the trade signs for tobacconists is the *Black*

Boy, which was certainly in use as a tobacco sign early in the seventeenth century, (it is mentioned in one of Ben Jonson's plays written in 1614), and for other purposes a good deal earlier. The association of ideas is of course with the natives of the region where tobacco was first discovered. As one might imagine, the sign-makers' idea of Caribbean natives varied considerably. Traditionally the figure is of a pot-bellied native with a skirt of tobacco leaves, and a crown. He holds under one arm a roll of tobacco, and in his other hand a long clay pipe. The crown as well as the skirt is of tobacco leaves (often taken for feathers). The earliest figures were very small – often no more than two feet tall – but eighteenth century examples were both taller and more western-ised, so that the 'black boy' became little more than a European man painted black. The extras (skirt and crown, tobacco roll and pipe) were almost invariable, however.

It is interesting to find that the Pipe Makers' Guild, which was incorporated in 1619, took as the supporters to its coat of arms 'two young moors all proper, wreathed about the loins with tobacco leaves vert', and the crest was also 'A Moor, in his dexter hand a tobacco pipe and in his sinister hand a roll of tobacco, all proper'. This does much to explain the variations in the figures used for this type of trade sign, for a 'Moor' was a generic term for almost any dark-skinned foreigner; even Edwardian children were brought up on the idea of a 'Blackamoor', an equally unspecific idea. So one finds that in the eighteenth century in particular, a wide variety of Eastern figures was also used to advertise tobacco-sellers. These were known as 'the Moor' or 'the Oriental'. 'The Turk' was another well-known eighteenth century sign, particularly in Scotland. At the beginning of this century at least, there were two examples in Edinburgh of 'Turks', one holding a long pipe and one a cheroot. Each wore a turban, long coat, baggy trousers and turned-up shoes. The pipe was a magnificent affair which stretched to the Turk's knees. Quite often the complete figure was reduced to a head, and the sign became 'The Black Boy's Head' or 'The Negro's Head' (which gave its name to a popular brand of tobacco), usually with a pipe between the teeth.

The *Red Indian* on the other hand has no connection with these variations of the Black Boy figure. Although the sign is scarcely known

Cigar store
Indian

in this country, it was universal in America from the eighteenth century onwards, and is generally known as a 'Cigar Store Indian'. Most were carved and painted. There is a fine example of one of these figures in the collection of the American Museum at Claverton Manor, near Bath.

An unusual type of eighteenth century tobacconist's sign was of *three hands* emerging from a single sleeve. One hand had a pinch of snuff on the thumb, the next held a pipe, and the last a bunch of tobacco leaves. Underneath was the following doggerel –

> *'We three are engaged in one cause;*
> *I snuffs, I smokes, I chaws'*

A variation of this sign was for the three hands to be replaced by painted figures of a Scotsman, a Dutchman and a sailor, with the same verse underneath.

A figure of a *Sailor* was used as a tobacconist's sign in some cases during the eighteenth century, particularly in seaports; he held a clay pipe in one hand. The sailor figure also was not uncommon as a pawn-broker's sign.

Tobacco pipe makers used one of two variations on the pipe theme to advertise their premises. The most usual was the *Three Pipes*, painted on a board. A large *Golden Pipe*, in iron or wood, was used to mark either a pipemaker or a tobacconist, and in some cases an iron-monger-tobacconist (it was not unusual for the two trades to be combined in one shop during the seventeenth and eighteenth centuries). 'Two' and 'Five' Tobacco Pipes were also known.

Other signboards used by tobacconists in the eighteenth century include the *Virginian* and the *Virginian Planter*, and – inevitably – *Sir Walter Raleigh*.

Another strange sign found in the eighteenth century is the *Abel Drugger*. Abel Drugger was a tobacconist character in Ben Jonson's play *The Alchemist*, written in 1610. Among the more unusual signs used by tobacconists was the *Green Man and Still*. The 'green man' was probably a mistaken attempt to copy the Indian which formed one of the supporters of the Distillers' Company arms; it was quite common for a tobacconist to trade as a distiller at the same time.

Snuff sellers almost invariably used a representation of a snuff

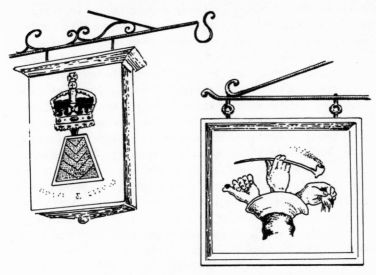

Trade signs – Three Hands and The Rasp and Crown

rasp, often in conjunction with some other symbol, as their trade sign. A common combination was the *Rasp and Crown*, and it was (and is) under this symbol that the celebrated snuff firm of Fribourg and Treyer traded from their shop in the Haymarket. The rasp is represented as an instrument shaped rather like a broad cricket bat, the 'blade' being a frame filled with cross-hatching. This type of rasp was used for the wholesale production of snuff. The cross-hatching indicates a perforated iron plate, across which the end of a thick roll of tobacco was rubbed. The Highlander figures already mentioned indicated a seller rather than a manufacturer of snuff, but it became so popular that it was used almost indiscriminately for snuff makers, snuff sellers and tobacconists before the end of the eighteenth century.

Trade Tokens

If anybody tried to produce his own coinage in present-day England, he would very rapidly be led away to a police court. The law was in force just the same during the seventeenth and eighteenth centuries, but there were good reasons why authority turned a blind eye to the very large amount of private coinage which was circulated. The most important was that the price of copper was often so high during this period that any copper coins struck by the Royal Mint would have been melted down and sold for more than their face value. The second reason was that when the Mint did strike copper coins of small denomination, the numbers were generally quite inadequate for the demand.

The first large-scale production of private coinage, or trade tokens as they are usually called, was at the beginning of the seventeenth century, partly as the result of the 'Harington farthings' struck by Lord Harington under Royal Warrant and much disliked by the people because they were so thin and small. Brass and pewter were the metals most commonly used. Many of the more substantial traders produced their own farthings and halfpennies, which were usually marked with their name and address and trade. The date was added, and often a representation of the trader's goods, or a copy of his trade sign. The British Museum has at least two examples of tobacconist's trade tokens from this period. One is a farthing issued by 'Alexander Sharp, in Chick Lane' which carries in the centre the sign of three pipes. The other is a heart-shaped halfpenny marked 'John Poyntting, in Cloath-fair (Smithfield)' on one side, and on the other 'his half penny 1667'; underneath is a tobacco roll. Another tobacconist, James Barnes, also traded in groceries as was common in 1659, when he issued a farthing token from the 'Sugar Loaf and Three Tobacco Rolls'. These tokens were accepted as legal currency by the public and other shopkeepers within the small area covered by the trader, which in the case of both these tokens was Smithfield.

These seventeenth century tokens are fairly rare. Their use was forbidden in 1672 by an Act of Charles II although one or two traders in remoter parts of the country continued to make and use them, and in Ireland they continued for another seven years. These seventeenth century tokens came in various shapes. The heart-shaped example has already been mentioned; lozenge, octagonal and square tokens were also produced. In size they were considerably smaller than the later issues; the halfpennies were roughly the size

Tobacconists' trade tokens

of a modern sixpence as a rule and the farthings smaller again.

The other large-scale production of trade tokens came at the end of the eighteenth century, as a result of the enormously increased number of wage-earners produced by the Industrial Revolution, and a simultaneous shortage of legal copper coinage. For about ten years from 1787, an enormous quantity of trade tokens was issued, mainly by industrial concerns but also by traders, particularly in London. Campbell's, a noted snuff and tobacco seller in Edinburgh, issued an extremely well-cast token showing the head of a Turk smoking a short curved clay pipe; round the edge were the words 'Payable at Campbell's Snuff Shop'. The reverse side was cast with a snuff jar and crossed pipes. The Georgian anti-smokers also made use of this opportunity for all-but-free advertising, by issuing a token showing tobacco being trampled underfoot and the words 'I will never use tobacco in any form'; and on the other side the following – 'Tobacco tends to idleness, poverty, strong drink, vice, ill-health, insanity and death'.

One bygone directly attributable to the use of trade tokens was the wooden box, divided into numerous compartments, which every trader had to keep on his premises. The tokens needed to be separated according to who had issued them, so that at the end of the month, or the year, they could be taken to him and exchanged for legal coinage.

Paper Ephemera

Among the minor products of the tobacco-trade which will interest the collector are several kinds of printed paper, including trade cards, bill-heads and tobacco papers. These were all intended to act as advertisements.

Trade cards and *bill heads* were often, during the seventeenth and eighteenth centuries, one and the same thing. A trader would keep on his counter a small pile of blank headed bills from which he would hand one to a customer as a reminder of his name and address. Hogarth spent a good deal of his time during his early days designing and engraving trade cards and bills for tradesmen of all kinds. He also did engravings for lampoons and satires against Sir Robert Walpole's Tobacco Excise Bill, introduced first in 1732. One of the Bill's greatest opponents was a tobacconist by the name of Ben Bradley, whose bill-head Hogarth engraved with a scene showing Britannia and the British Lion both happily smoking their pipes.

Some of the very fine engraved bill-heads which survive from the mid-eighteenth century show how many Frenchmen had come to England to introduce to new customers the habit of snuffing – 'John L. Hullier, French manufacturer of Rapée snuff, formally inspector general of all the manufacturers of snuff in France': and 'John Saulle and Pontet, successors to the late James Fribourg . . .'; or Abraham Delvalle; who 'makes and sells at his manufactory in Featherstone Street, Burnhill Fields, fine Scotch, Rapée, Spanish and Havannah Snuffs'.

These bill-heads also show how varied was the trade carried on by a tobacconist, who sold groceries, or sweets, or liquor, or spices, as he wished. There is nothing strange in this to the modern smoker, of course, who buys his cigarettes at a newsagent or a sweet-shop, or a public house, or a supermarket. The difference is that in the seventeenth and eighteenth centuries, the selling of tobacco was the prime reason for the shop's existence.

From the middle of the seventeenth century, *tobacco papers* (in which loose tobacco was wrapped for the purchaser in the shop) began to be decorated, usually with roughly printed rhymes, or with representations of the shop sign under which the trade was conducted. The rhymes themselves were usually crude (from the literary, not the moral, point of view): for example –

> *Here's two full boxes, taste which you think right,*
> *The one's to smoak, the other's to clear the sight;*
> *I do declare they're both the very best;*
> *Then pray confess I'm the Tobacconist.*

Some rather special tobacco-papers were used by an American tobacconist in 1748, who managed to get hold of a captured Spanish ship-load of Papal Bulls; and he advertised them 'at a much cheaper rate than they can be purchased of the French and Spanish priests, and yet will be warranted to be of the same advantage to the possessors.'

A very popular fashion for tobacco-papers was the printing on them of puzzles reminiscent of the 'mottoes' in Christmas crackers. Among these doggerels of the eighteenth century are many which conceal moral and uplifting messages when deciphered. The deciphering was usually no more than the reading of the rhyme backwards, or the rearrangement of mutilated words. The following example from a mid-eighteenth century tobacco paper could well have been taken from a modern cracker, but for the reference to types of tobacco:

> *O and P ran a race; Q backed O, knowing that P would win. Why*
> *was this like going into a shop and asking for 'shag' and getting*
> *'short-cut?'*
> *Because it was wrong 'to back O'.*

Many tobacco papers were designed as pure advertisements. An interesting example, engraved in about 1780, shows a picture of three gentlemen. The first, an Englishman, holds out a twist of tobacco and says 'Will you have a Quid'. The next, a Dutchman smoking a short clay, says 'No, Dis been Better', and the third, a Frenchman with sword, wig, tricorn and snuff-box, offers the latter saying 'Voulez-vous de Rappé'.

It was fashionable among London tobacco sellers in the early eighteenth century for pages from books to be used as tobacco papers. Addison remarked, on this, 'For as no mortal author, in the ordinary fate and vicissitude of things, knows to what use his works may, some time or other be applied, a man may often meet with very celebrated names in a paper of tobacco. I have lighted my pipe more than once with the writings of a prelate'.

Cigar Labels

Another by-product of the tobacco industry which became very popular as a collector's item was the cigar label – known now as the 'band'. These began to be put on cigars in the eighteen fifties when large imports of Havana cigars started. They lack the appeal of cigarette cards or matchbox labels because they were nothing but advertisements for the makers and have little or no pictorial merit. Nevertheless they were collected by many people. One extraordinary fashion which came from this collecting was the sticking of cigar labels on to china plates, completely covering them. This was something of a craze towards the end of the nineteenth century and the collector may well find examples of this strange art in a junk shop.

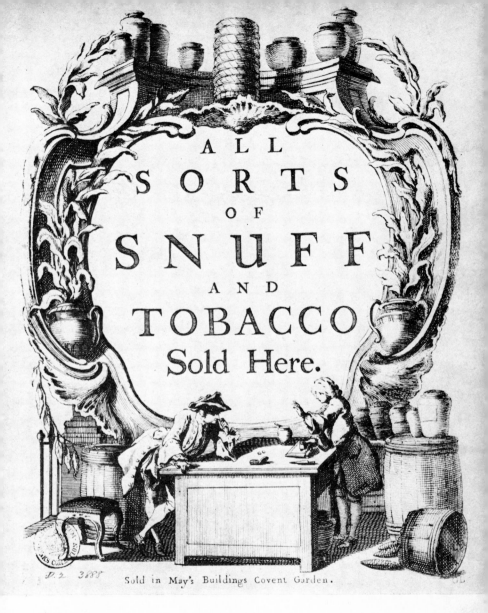

ALL
SORTS
OF
SNUFF
AND
TOBACCO
Sold Here.

Sold in May's Buildings Covent Garden.

Eighteenth century tobacconist's trade-card.
Lead tobacco jar and late nineteenth century decorative match containers
(*see over*).

A selection of eighteenth and nineteenth century tobacconists' trade-cards and letter headings.

9. Dress and Furniture

It must be remembered that smoking anywhere except in places set aside for the purpose (and there were few of these apart from the inns, which no gentleman could frequent) was very much frowned upon in the Victorian era, mainly because the Queen herself hated tobacco. Smoking was not allowed in the London clubs until White's broke with tradition in 1845, bowing to the demands of the younger members. Until then, as it was impossible to smoke in the club and unheard-of to smoke in the street, the most daring club members occupied no-man's-land and were to be seen smoking on the club steps. Thackeray, in his *Book of Snobs* published in 1846, speaks of 'that den of abomination, which, I am told, has been established in *some* clubs, called the *"Smoking Room"*'. H. J. Nellar in his *Nicotiana*, written fourteen years earlier, mentions the Cigar Divans which had frequently sprung up in London to provide somewhere for a gentleman to smoke his cigar in peace and reasonable luxury. They were furnished in elaborate Eastern style, and Turkish coffee was served to the clients who lay back on comfortable couches. At least one of these Cigar Divans, of which there were something like a dozen in London by the time Queen Victoria came to the throne in 1837, was still in existence when she died in 1901.

In the home, tobacco was limited entirely to one special room of the house (it was also permitted in the billiard-room, provided that it was nowhere near any other room used by ladies).

The preface to Thackeray's *Fitzboodle Papers* says 'no gentleman in those days was seen smoking even a "weed" in the streets'. Cigarettes were practically unheard of in England, and outside one's private smoking room pipes were tabooed. Men in Society slunk into their smoking-rooms, or, when there was no smoking-room, into the kitchen or servants' hall, after the domestic staff had retired. A smoking jacket was worn in the place of their ordinary evening coat, and their well-oiled, massive head of hair was protected by a gorgeously decorated 'smoking-cap'.

Smoking Jackets

Smoking cap and jacket

Smoking Jackets were handsome pieces of clothing. Velvet was the most usual material, but they were also made of plush, cashmere, and flannel, lined with brightly coloured silk. The traditional embellishment was the brandenburg, or military frogging, and large oval buttons known as 'olives'.

A remarkable advertisement appeared in newspapers just before the Great War, as follows:- . . . 'the well-dressed woman has begun to consider the little smoking jacket indispensable'. It was apparently 'a very different matter to the braided velvet coats which were donned by our masculine forebears in the days of long drooping cavalry moustaches, tightly buttoned frock coats, and flexible canes. The feminine smoking jacket of today is worn with entrancing little evening or semi-evening frocks . . . ' Whatever the result of this appeal, the Great War produced a new kind of woman who needed no excuses of this kind to please herself about smoking wherever she wanted.

Smoking Caps

With the smoking jacket (at least the male variety) went the Smoking Cap, a round velvet pillbox almost invariably decorated with a long tassel. Smoking caps were a favourite present from adoring womenfolk, who spent many careful hours embroidering these symbols of subordination. Equally popular with Victorian womenfolk was the making and embroidering of *tobacco slippers* – designed not for wear but for hanging on the wall of the smoking room, filled with tobacco.

Tobacco Pouches

The tobacco pouch was a Victorian invention, and one which suffered the extremes of decoration at the hands of the smoker's womenfolk. Fairholt, writing in 1876, says 'Tobacco when carried about the person for use, if not placed in a metal box, is held in a pouch or bag; both being generally formed of leather. German ladies think it no unfit employ to devote much time and attention in embroidering tobacco bags for favoured swains . . . . Gentlemen hang the tobacco bag on the arm, as ladies used the reticule some time ago'. Most gentlemen, however, preferred not to flaunt gaudy tobacco bags on their arms, but to carry it in a leather pouch in their pockets.

Snuff Handkerchiefs

Whatever the addicts may say, the sniffing up of powdered tobacco into one's nose is a dirty habit if one cares to consider it dispassionately; and when (as frequently happens, particularly to the inexperienced snuffer) this causes a sneeze, then the sneezer should take precautions. This was recognised even in the eighteenth century, when people were a good deal less particular than they are now. Special snuff handkerchiefs were sold by the leading snuff-makers. They were used not only to catch sneezes and to blow noses, but more particularly to protect the snuffers' clothes, especially the white stock which he wore round his neck. They were large – about two feet square – and for obvious reasons were also coloured, rather than white. Messrs Fribourg and Treyer (who still sell snuff handkerchiefs to this day) were selling them at 28s a dozen at the end of the eighteenth century. They were usually printed with designs showing popular ballads or scenes of London life. The modern snuff handkerchiefs have designs of Fribourg and Treyer's shop, with the names of the varieties of snuff they sell.

Snuff Waistcoats

Real addicts in the eighteenth century even went to the length of having special snuff waistcoats made, with very large flapped pockets to contain their snuff box (or boxes, for some confirmed snuff takers would carry two or three different kinds to suit their mood, or the weather, or the time of day, or their surroundings). As is mentioned elsewhere, Dr Johnson went to the other extreme and carried large quantities of snuff loose in his pockets.

Spittoons

There is, of course, another way of using tobacco apart from smoking it or sniffing it. It can be chewed. This is probably how it was first enjoyed for its mild narcotic effect and for the way it helped the chewer to forget his hunger. In this country, chewing has for the last hundred years at least been confined in the public's mind to seamen. It was not always so. In the middle of the eighteenth century, it was quite the thing among the more extreme of young men of fashion to chew tobacco rather than to use snuff (which this particular set regarded as effete and womanish; there is still an undercurrent of this feeling today). The tobacco-seller's trade-card showing the three types of tobacco user – the chewer, the smoker and the snuffer – has already been mentioned.

The chewing of tobacco was quite permissible among gentlemen in the seventeenth as well as the eighteenth century. General Monk, at the time of the Restoration of Charles II, was a confirmed tobacco-chewer, and his lead was followed by many others. It was the custom for tobacco chewers, among courtiers at least, to carry a small silver spittoon, in form indistinguishable from a porringer or the Scottish quaitch. An engraving of such a Cavalier spitting elegantly into his silver bowl is shown by Fairholt. His illustration was taken from the lid of a snuff rasp.

Spittoons for tobacco chewers (and quite as much for the smokers of foul clay pipes) continued to be made until the 1890's, in spite of the shudders of successive generations of ladies. In the authors' collection is an example in glazed brown stoneware clay, clearly intended for use in a public house, and made probably in about 1850. As late as 1861, spittoons of wood, triangular in shape and filled with sawdust, were part of the normal furnishings of the pews in at least one Essex church. In the tap-room of inns too, spittoons were a necessary part of the scene.

The common pattern for a floor-standing spittoon was a circular metal or china pan. Some were much more elaborate, however – moulded stoneware examples decorated with shells (probably for inn tap-rooms) were made in the eighteen fifties; elaborate painted and gilded ones for the tastefully-furnished home in the sixties; and

Stoneware spittoon

the eighties produced the crowning glory, in the shape of the 'Salivarium', which was a spittoon disguised as a footstool, complete with beaded cover on a frame of walnut, oak or mahogany.

Smokers' Chairs

In the late eighteen nineties, the comfort of the Victorian father, happily shut away in his smoking room, wearing his smoking jacket and his smoking cap, was further ensured by the introduction of the smoker's chair.

Illustrations of designs in 'Furniture and Decoration' of February 1897 show that they came in several different forms – heavily upholstered in buttoned leather for prolonged comfort, or severely upright and hard for the quick and conscience-ridden puff. The essential feature of all designs was a drawer under the seat, containing a spittoon. The drawer was on springs, so that it could be pulled out by means of the cord attached, and slid away automatically when the cord was released.

Victorian smoker's chair

Spill Vases

Every household, from medieval times until at least the beginning
of our own century, kept a supply of spills, usually slivers of wood,
in a container close to the fire, so that lamps or candles could be
lit. These spill containers were made in every possible material –
wrought iron, leather, wood, brass and copper, glass, china. It
was not until the Victorian era that they began to be made primarily
as decorative pieces to beautify the mantlepiece. Probably the most
common are the glazed pottery vases about six inches high, decorated
very often in garish colours and gilding, and with a country or military
scene painted on the side. These are often found in pairs.

Spill vase

Spillcutters

Spill cutting machines were, during much of the nineteenth century, a standard piece of equipment in every inn. They worked on exactly the same principle as the smoothing plane, and consisted of a piece of iron mounted on a heavy wooden block. The top of the iron was formed into a channel and near one end was a projecting steel cutting edge, which could be adjusted in the same way as the blade of a plane. If a block of soft wood was pushed along the channel into the blade, a thin spiral was cut off. Some models were fitted with a drawer in the base to hold the blocks of wood. An inn-keeper would usually prepare enough to fill a spill-vase or two, and then leave his customers to cut their own when the supply was exhausted.

Spill cutter

Ashtrays

With very few exceptions, the ashtray has little of interest to offer the collector. Since the introduction of the cigarette, every suitable material has been made use of to fashion a dish to keep the ash off the carpet. The eighteenth century 'Smoker's Companion' pipe-burner mentioned on page 46 was provided with an ashtray, however, and this must have been one of the early examples. Another interesting item of the same period was the smoker's ashes pan, a copper bowl on three or four legs, which was provided with a wooden handle, for easy passing between pipe smokers.

10. Cigars

It seems to have been in the form of cigars that Europeans first met the use of tobacco, when Columbus' companions landed in the West Indies in 1492. But it was a very long time before cigar smoking came to Europe. The primitive cigars smoked by the Indians at the time of Columbus' landings were rolls of palm leaf containing dried tobacco. This was gradually improved to become a roll of tobacco leaves pierced down the centre by a straw. This form of tobacco-smoking remained, in general, in those parts of South America which were conquered by the Spaniards. With the returning conquerors, cigars came to Spain. The origin of the word 'cigar' (used by an Englishman as early as 1735) is probably from the Spanish *cigarar,* to roll, although one school of thought prefers the Spanish *cigarrel,* an orchard, from the idea that the first cigars were smoked in an orchard. This sounds suspiciously like a manufactured derivation, however.

In about the middle of the eighteenth century, the new habit began to spread slowly through Europe, ousting as it went the firmly-entrenched habit of snuff-taking. It was the Peninsular War, however, when Napoleon was fighting through Spain and England was trying to stop him, that brought cigars to the notice of the public in this country. Isolated imports of cigars had certainly been made into England before the beginning of the nineteenth century, by travellers who had acquired a liking for them abroad. But after the peace of 1815, the veterans of the Spanish campaign came home in their thousands, bringing with them a firm and insatiable taste for the cigar. This taste must have been satisfied very largely by secret imports, for although duty on imported cigars after 1815 was fixed at 18s per lb, in 1823, eight years later, only 26 lbs of cigars were officially imported. By 1830, however, the figure was 253,822 lbs.

It should not be thought that the cigars of 1815, or of several decades afterwards, were the fat, country-sausage shaped affairs we know today. Early nineteenth century cigars were small, hard and strong, much nearer in fact to the modern cheroot – a word which was invented by the Portuguese in India in about 1670. The difference between a cheroot and a cigar, by the way, is that the former is always cut flat at both ends, and these days is made mechanically by rolling tobacco on to a wire.

The first cigars to be made in Europe were called 'tobacco sticks', and they were manufactured by a German in Italy from 1779. Another German opened the first factory devoted to cigars in 1788, in Hamburg. The story, told by Count Corti in his *History of Smoking*, is that Herr Schlottmann, the founder of the factory, found that his home-made cigars were not at first popular in competition with those shipped from Havana. He accordingly sent them from Hamburg to Cuxhaven, put them on an American ship sailing back to Hamburg and unloaded them again, whereupon they sold readily as 'genuine imported'.

When cigars came to England after 1815, they became so popular that in the course of the following twenty years snuff-taking, which had practically ousted pipe-smoking, almost died out itself. In 1829 the duty on cigars was lowered to 9s per lb, half what it had been, and everyone took to cigar smoking. For the first time, special smoking rooms were set apart at the House of Commons, in the face of disapproval in some very high places. Queen Victoria, who came to the throne in 1837, loathed tobacco in any form and the Duke of Wellington (whose own troops brought the cigar habit to England) was another powerful figure in the anti-tobacco world. In 1845 he issued an order to the Army in the following terms:

The Commander-in-Chief has been informed that the practice of smoking, by the use of pipes, cigars or cheroots, has become prevalent among the officers of the Army, which is not only in itself a species of intoxication occasioned by the fumes of tobacco, but, undoubtedly, occasions drinking and tippling by those who acquire the habit .... and he intreats the officers commanding regiments to prevent smoking in the mess rooms .... and to discourage the practice among the officers of Junior Rank in their regiments.

Cigar Cases

In spite of opposition – and how often one has to use this phrase in telling the story of tobacco! – cigar smoking spread until it became the standard form of enjoying tobacco. Smokers soon found that carrying their cigars loose in the pocket was good neither for the cigars nor their clothes, and from about 1845 onwards large numbers of specially-made cases were produced for the pocket. The problem of keeping the cigars themselves in good condition was not a serious one, for the English have always been accused of liking dry cigars and damp pipe tobacco, in direct contrast to the rest of the smoking world. Cases were made in a great variety of material and shape and to suit all tastes and financial circumstances. A popular and early form was a wooden case in the shape of a book, one half sliding over the other.

Other cases were veneered in woods typical of the Regency period, including rosewood and amboyna. Later in the century, large numbers of plain wooden pocket cigar cases were decorated with the enormously popular black transfer-printed scenes, and also with tartan patterns. Many of these were made in Scotland, where they were known as 'magazines'. Leather was extremely popular, and a cheap form of case in moulded hide was produced in quantity from about 1850. Leather cigar cases were often decorated with tooling or gilding.

Although some examples, particularly towards the end of the nineteenth century when elaborate decoration had got beyond the bounds of taste or even sense, are so embellished with medallions, embroidery, mother-of-pearl, carvings and so on, that it might otherwise be difficult to recognise them for what they are, the lingering smell of cigars is an unmistakeable pointer. Many more expensive cases of the same period were designed to combine other uses with cigar storage; pockets for visiting cards or photographs, and compartments for cigar-holders and match boxes are all to be found built into cigar cases.

Although the shape of cigars and the primary purpose of a case – to keep the contents flat and uncrushed – meant that cigar cases had to be basically oblong, every possible alternative was exploited in such details as the method of opening. A popular type was hinged along the side and opened like a book, the cigars being ranged four or five to each leaf; the two sides were held together by a spring catch when closed. Some particularly attractive specimens of this kind were made both in tortoiseshell and in ivory. Probably the most popular among the cheaper forms of case was the type in which an inner container slid into an outer sheath of identical shape. These were made in leather (and imitation leather), wood, tortoiseshell, straw marquetry mounted on cardboard, and particularly in papier mâché.

This last material was especially popular in the period immediately before and after the Great Exhibition of 1851, and it was found to be as ideal for cigar cases as it had been for snuff boxes – it was cheap to manufacture, excellent as a surface for painted decoration, reasonably durable, and had good insulating properties which helped to keep

Papier Mâché cigar cases

cigars in good condition. Although many different patterns of papier mâché pocket cases were made, there is one type which should be mentioned particularly, if only because they are often confused with spectacle cases.

These are about six inches long and up to three inches wide, D-ended and are constructed from two leaves of papier mâché joined at the sides by means of leather gussets. There was always a separate internal case of thin leather or stiff cardboard, which slid into the outer case from one end, but this is often missing. When empty, the case is quite flat as the leather gussets allow the two outer leaves to fall together. This feature, together with the presence of the internal case and the small size of the whole container (suited of course to the small cheroots popular at the time) has led to the confusion with spectacle cases.

One or both of the outer papier mâché leaves of the case, and very occasionally part of the inner case as well, was invariably decorated in oil paint. The subjects were usually portraits (mostly pretty girls) and country or domestic scenes. The execution was, on the whole, crude, but the effect is charming. Other subjects in the authors' collection are a coat-of-arms of the Ancient Order of Foresters; bull-fighting scenes; Taglioni in her rôle of La Sylphide, and Jenny Lind the 'Swedish Nightingale'; and a combination of popular appeal and good advertising in the form of a pretty girl wrapping up cigars at a counter. This particular example is titled 'La Marchande de Cigarres', but evidence (including a grammatical error in the French caption of another example in the authors' collection) suggests that all these cases were made in Germany at a single factory, and that the manufacturers paid a good deal of attenion to their export trade. German, English, French, Spanish and Swiss scenes are all included in the output. It is rare, but not unknown, for both leaves of the papier mâché to be decorated in this way. In most examples, the second leaf is patterned on the background in gold on black with a microbe-like decoration over the whole surface. Occasionally, the word 'cigars', or 'cegars', is painted in the middle of the leaf.

Some cases otherwise similar but made of metal are also known; these were obviously produced by the same establishment.

Noteworthy among the colossal output of cigar cases in the late Victorian period are the soft cloth cases heavily embroidered by loving hands with beadwork patterns or silk pictures. These pouches were never intended to leave the smoking room, and were inseparable companions of the smoking jacket and cap described earlier.

Cigar Dispensers

In the course of the eighteenth century, some attractive semi-mechanical cigar cabinets, designed to stand on a table or desk, were

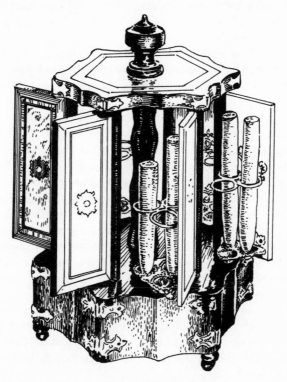

Cigar dispenser

made – predecessors of the many similar cigarette dispensers of the early years of our own century. The Pinto collection has at least two of these, both similar in principle and about nine inches high, made probably between 1830 and 1840. A knob on the top of the miniature cabinet opens all the six doors, behind five of which is a holder for cigars, and behind the sixth a piercer, match holder and striker. Both examples are lavishly decorated, one by means of veneers of fine woods and ormolu, and the other hand-painted with flowers on an ebonised mahogany base. Another type of novelty cigar dispenser of the mid-nineteenth century looked, when closed, like a wooden pillar about ten inches high and six inches wide, surmounted by a small eggcup, the whole formed from mahogany. In the 'eggcup' was a catch, which when released allowed the lid of the hollow pillar to rise on a column, bringing with it a dozen or so cigars in wire holders, which fanned out as they rose. A remarkably elaborate way of keeping and presenting a cigar, one would have thought, and much more of a novelty than the equipment of a serious cigar-smoker.

Cigar Holders

The controversy as to whether a cigarette tastes better when smoked in a holder or without it seems to have died away in our day; one sees few holders in use at all events. The same argument raged about cigars in the eighteen forties and fifties. The answer in both cases was probably that it does not matter in the slightest. Some nineteenth century experts maintained, however, that a holder was essential because all the narcotics formed by the burning tobacco condensed in the last inch of the cigar, which therefore got more and more rank the further it was smoked. Whatever the reason, if one wants to make an effect a holder is a very useful accessory. The difference between cigar holders (or cigar tubes as they were originally called) of the Victorian era and cigarette holders of the period after the First World War is that the former could be a great deal more ornate and still fit into the contemporary scene. Even allowing for this some extraordinary examples were produced.

The earliest cigar holders were probably straight tubes of clay, and the French factories which specialised in clay pipes turned out some very fine decorated examples. The most favoured of later holders were meerschaum ones, which followed the fashions of meerschaum pipes already mentioned, and which were made very largely in Austria, Germany and France. Vienna was the most important centre of production. Some exquisite examples of the carver's art were produced for the purpose, the range of subjects being almost unlimited. It would seem that the skill of 'colouring' a meerschaum cigar holder would have been more difficult than in the case of a pipe, but in some examples it seems to have been achieved with equal success. Some meerschaum cigar holders are

Meerschaum cigar holders

basically straight tubes, so that the cigar is in the same line as the holders; the carving is usually confined in this type to a figure or animal on top of the tube. Others are made in the form of a gentle S-curve, down from the mouthpiece and up to the cigar, which projects at a jaunty angle. Still others are miniature pipes, the cigar sticking up vertically from the bowl.

The straight tube, simple and unadorned except for perhaps a gold band between holder and mouthpiece, remains popular to this day. It was made in many different materials – amber, semi-precious stones, polished wood, jet, porcelain, and even glass. Some very ornate (and, one would have thought, highly delicate) glass holders were made in the second half of the nineteenth century, mostly in the form of straight tubes but some in the shape of miniature pipes. They derived their decorative effect partly from the use of different coloured glasses and partly from applied glass mouldings. Some holders were also made in cut glass. Whatever the decorative merits of these glass cigar holders (and they were on the whole over-ornate) they must have been uncomfortable to use, and it seems likely that they were largely intended as novelties to be classed with other glass 'fairings' turned out by the thousand in many of our famous glass factories.

Among the more extraordinary fashions in holders was the use of bird and animal bones during the last decade of the nineteenth century. The art was to leave the bones (even skulls were used) as much in the natural state as possible, making use of their existing features for mouthpiece and bowl. Sometimes bones were added to in meerschaum or gold or other materials.

Another class of late nineteenth century holder was of a completely different pattern. It was bought in the form of a 'bowl' only, and was completed by inserting a narrow wooden tube into a small hole at the back. The lack of a stem in the design allowed the makers of these novelties to give free rein to their imaginations. A popular model in meerschaum was the bust of a gentleman complete with top hat, monocle and whiskers.

A holder of about 1870 illustrated by Fairholt was designed to act simply as a gripper. It is hard to see the advantage of this, as it did no more than save the finger and thumb the burden of keeping themselves closed round the cigar. The other end is fashioned into a cigar cutter in the form of two sharpened crescents. The instrument could be hung from a watch chain. The whole thing has a vague air of the Gothic about it.

Cigar Mould

A wooden instrument which was not made in this country, but which could prove puzzling to a collector if it turned up, was the multiple cigar mould, used in America during the late nineteenth century when cheap cigars were made by this combination of hand and mass-production methods. It consists of no more than two boards hinged together, in each of which is carved a series of depressions shaped to half a cigar. Each side was filled with tobacco and the mould shut and pegged to produce a cigar ready for wrapping (for the tobacco of a good cigar is in two quite distinct parts – the interior and the wrapper. Many plantations grow nothing but tobacco destined for use as wrapper leaf).

Cigar-smoking Companion

Fairholt, writing in 1875, illustrates in his *'History of Tobacco'* a pocket-knife designed exclusively for the cigar smoker. It is really a kind of 'companion'. At one end is a hole into which the tip of the cigar may be put for cutting when the end of the closed blade is pushed down; and one side of the handle is divided into two boxes with hinged lid – one holding fusees and the other tinder.

Cigar Cutters

There are, and have been ever since the first cigars arrived in this country, several different schools of thought as to the right way to deal with the end of a cigar to make sure that it draws properly. For each of these schools, a different instrument was made. When one also remembers that the mid-Victorians loved to disguise things so that they looked like something else altogether, it will be realised that cigar-cutters (we use the word 'cutter' for the sake of simplicity to include piercers and nickers) may be found in an astonishing range of shapes.

Probably the largest group of cigar smokers was the one which liked to cut a small slice from the end of the cigar. This could be done, and often was, with a small, very sharp, knife, but for less adept smokers a selection of special cutters were made. So varied are the designs that it is worth inspecting almost any piece of nineteenth century metal-work or woodwork for a small round hole and a lever or button nearby which brings a sharpened blade across the hole (into which the end of the cigar was pushed). The Pinto collection has a

Mephistopholean head in painted wood, the mouth taking the end of the cigar and a lever under the chin working the blade; and a barrel where the tap on the bung moves the cutter. Most cutters designed for the pocket are comparatively straightforward metal objects not unlike modern nail-clippers, occasionally incorporating two or three weapons for dealing with the end of the cigar.

The next group of cigar smokers preferred a V-shaped nick in the end of their cigars. What is required here is a cup-shaped receptacle into which the end of the cigar fits, and a sharpened steel blade of the right shape hinged to the body of the cutter. Again, an enormous number of different designs were made. The authors have recently found a very handsome dog's head in white metal, into the end of which is hinged the V-shaped blade.

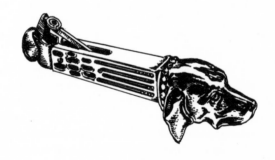

Cigar cutter

Finally, cutters which pierced rather than cut the cigar were also popular. Some pierced from the side, and some through the end down the length of the cigar. The simplest and earliest of this type is a plain silver pin in a small case.

Although the Havana cigar for which all these instruments were designed appeared in Britain in about the middle of the nineteenth century, a very large proportion of the 'novelty' cigar cutters were made in this century – most of them, in fact, in the last thirty years.

11. Cigarettes

The date of the first appearance of the cigarette in Europe is not known, partly because it is impossible to decide when the word started to mean the sort of cigarette we know today; it was occasionally used to describe very small cigars in the late Georgian period. On the other hand, Casanova recorded in his memoirs having seen 'cigarettes of Brazilian tobacco wrapped in a paper tube' being smoked; and this was in 1769. Whatever the true date of their introduction to Europe, cigarettes certainly came, like tobacco itself, from South America. They had reached France by 1844 and were seen and remarked upon in England during the first half of the nineteenth century. But it was invariably a foreigner, or an Englishman who had travelled extensively on the Continent, who did the smoking. The home-keeping Englishman was firmly attached to his cigar.

America took to the cigarette a year or two before England did, mainly because of the large mixed immigrant population streaming to her democratic shores at this time. By 1854 in fact, a certain Mr Robert of New York was able to observe that 'Some of the *ladies* of this refined and fashion-forming metropolis are aping the ways of some pseudo-accomplished foreigners in smoking tobacco through a weaker and more *feminine* article which has been most delicately denominated *cigarette*'. This feeling died hard, for Ouida, in one of her novels, was shivering delicately at the idea of one of her lady characters smoking a cigarette as late as 1870. Wolf-Ferrari's charming little opera, *Susanna's Secret*, set at the turn of the century, revolves upon the secret cigarettes enjoyed by its heroine.

Once again, it was a war that changed our habits. The Peninsular

War brought us the cigar and the Crimean War the cigarette. The Crimean War of 1853–6, fought by the Russians on one side and the Turks, British, French and Sardinians on the other was, apart from the fearful casualties caused by neglect of wounds (which persisted until Miss Nightingale arrived), an excellent opportunity for five ill-assorted nations to marvel at each other's strange habits, and acquire those it thought might be useful or amusing. The soldiers from England were quick to discover how much cheaper it was to roll these handy little paper tubes of tobacco instead of buying ready-made cigars. The Turks and Russians in particular had been smoking cigarettes for many years at this date, and the habit was almost universal among them. A certain R. P. Gloag, who had gone to the Crimea as Paymaster to the Turkish forces decided to exploit this newly-acquired taste on his return to England and set up a factory at Walworth in 1857.

Gloag's cigarettes were very different from their modern descendants. They were of course hand-made, about five inches long, half as long again as ours, and twice as thick. The paper in which the tobacco was wrapped was coarse and yellow, and the tobacco itself was extremely strong. Finally each cigarette came with a mouthpiece or holder made of straw already attached. Officers home from the Crimea patronised Mr Gloag, but the vast majority of the soldiers and sailors who had acquired the habit continued to make their own, using coarse pipe tobacco (known as 'canister') and any paper that came to hand.

Fairholt describes cigarette papers which could be bought in the 1870's – 'porous like India paper and smouldering without smoke. The best is made at Valencia, and is sold for the sake of such persons as may wish to cut up their own tobacco and form cigarettes, in small books, bound in a coloured or plain cover, and from which a leaf, sufficient to form a cigarette, may be torn as wanted'. A desirable collector's item, and one which the authors, at least, have never seen for sale.

In Austria in 1865, what became a very popular type of cigarette was introduced. It was three times as long as a modern cigarette, had a cane mouthpiece at each end, and had to be cut in half before being smoked.

Edwardian combined pipe, cigar holder and cigarette holder

As the years went by and competition in making and selling cigarettes became fiercer, some extraordinary varieties appeared on the market – cigarettes with edible mouthpieces and telescopic mouthpieces; cigarettes impregnated with scent, coloured cigarettes to match ladies' dresses (these have of course now returned in the guise of 'cocktail' cigarettes); and filter-tips in which the charcoal filter was contained in a separate glass mouthpiece. These filters were designed not so much to preserve the health of the smoker as to prevent the smell of tobacco on his – and particularly on *her* – breath; and to make absolutely sure, a packet of strongly-flavoured sweets was given away with every packet. Other shots in the trade war were cigarettes made to appeal to pipe smokers by having a wooden plug inserted into the end of the tobacco, just in front of the cane mouthpiece, so it could 'be bitten on – like a pipe', as the makers advertised.

Until well after the turn of the century, Gloag's cigarettes were still sold complete with mouthpiece. He introduced a new kind of material for his mouthpieces every few years – vulcanite in 1897, cherrywood in 1905.

The sliding-tray cigarette packet (which now seems to be going out of fashion again in favour of the squarer uncrushable packet) was imported in about 1887 by an American, James Duke.

The early 1870's saw the introduction of the modern cigarette, using the much milder Virginian tobacco and special fine white paper. In the year 1900 it was estimated that four-fifths of the tobacco consumed in Britain was burned in pipes and one-fifth in cigarettes, though W. A. Penn writing in 1901, said that '20 years ago the cigarette was almost unknown outside France, Spain, Italy and Turkey. Today it is the most popular smoke among all classes in England and America'. Fifty years later, the figures were reversed.

Cigarette Holders

Cigarette holders certainly go back to Gloag's original cigarettes, each one supplied with its own mouthpiece of straw or cane. By 1900, after the introduction of the much finer Virginian tobacco, superfine cigarette paper and packing by machines, the holder seems to have gone somewhat out of fashion. Sir Henry Thompson invented one in 1900 which contained a pad of cotton wool 'to absorb the oils'. He goes on to say with alarming assurance 'smoked simply, or with cotton-wool interposed, I do not hesitate to regard the cigarette as the least potent, and therefore the least injurious, form of tobacco-smoking'. Perhaps the inhaling of cigarette smoke was the exception rather than the rule.

W. A. Penn writing in 1901 recommends that a sort of home-made tip to a cigarette should be made by running 'a burning wax vesta round the end, thinly coating it with wax to form a mouthpiece. This is tasteless, efficient, non-absorbent, and equal to the amber-tipped cigarettes, which are prepared by coating one end with spermaceti'.

Most of the extravagant cigarette holders that one might come across were made in the period between the end of the Great War and

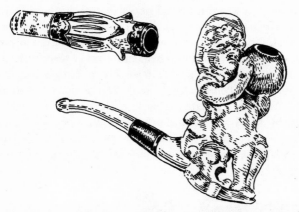

Meerschaum cigarette holders

the Slump. The yard-long holder was almost the trade-mark of the 'flapper'. There was also a fashion at about the same time for making cigarette holders in the form of miniature pipes, so that the cigarette pointed up into air instead of being a continuation of the tube.

Many cigarette holders followed exactly the materials and patterns of the cigar holders they replaced. Particularly attractive were some of the meerschaum holders, which are only distinguishable from their elder brothers by the size of the hole at the end.

Cigarette-making Machines

One of the few nineteenth century bygones connected with cigarettes is the forerunner of the modern pocket cigarette-making machine. This consisted of a mould in the form of a wooden tube, slightly tapered, a funnel and a ramrod. The three parts could be fitted together into a compact pencil-sized whole when not required. The wooden mould was used with a special thin paper tube sold in packets with the apparatus. To make a cigarette, one of the brown paper tubes was placed inside the mould, the little funnel filled with tobacco applied to the projecting end, and the ramrod used to push the tobacco firmly down until the tube was filled. The taper of the tube was necessary to avoid the filled paper getting stuck inside because of too-enthusiastic ramming. Such machines were made in the 1870's and probably originated in France, where most of the advances in tobacco consumption of the nineteenth century seem to have come from. (Incidentally, the British aversion to French tobacco goes back a long way. Penn in 1901, said 'France has no more terrible weapon than her cigarette'). Few Englishmen could make a good cigarette by hand at the turn of the century, by which time the yellow paper tube had been replaced by the wafer-thin rice-paper, an advance which made the cigarette-making tube described above quite impracticable.

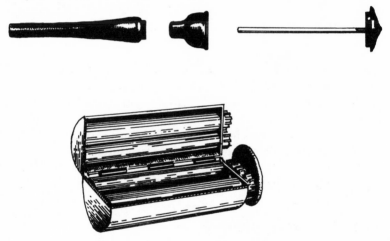

Two early cigarette making machines

The forerunner of the modern hand cigarette-making machine (which rolls the tobacco on a small endless belt) appeared soon afterwards. It was a metal cylinder about three and a half inches long, divided lengthwise into two halves and lined with meshing cogs running the length of the cylinder. The paper was laid on the cogs, filled with tobacco, and the two halves closed. A wheel at one end of the cylinder wrapped the paper round the tobacco, and the two halves of the machine were opened to disclose something approximately like a cigarette.

Cigarette Cases

Pocket cases and boxes for holding cigarettes were made from the time that manufactured cigarettes appeared in this country (1857) and have not changed radically since then. During the 1920's and 30's there was a vogue for cases made of figured birchwood with wooden hinges based upon Laurencekirk boxes (see under 'SNUFF'). One interesting collector's item which is not infrequently to be found in second-hand shops is the brass box which was sent to all the British troops for Christmas 1914 by the then Princess Mary. The lid of the box, about six inches by three, is impressed with a medallion of the princess and the name of the allies – Belgium, Japan, Russia, Serbia and France – and the date, and contained chocolate and cigarettes as well as a little card wishing the recipients 'A Victorious New Year'.

Princess Mary's brass gift box

Cigarette Stands

During the 1930's there was a considerable production of elaborate semi-mechanical cigarette stands, in the form of wooden cabinets with doors which opened when a knob, often disguised, was turned. These were developments of very similar cigar cabinets, mostly continental, which had been fashionable about a hundred years previously. Some of them were extremely intricate, displaying the cigarettes in fans and other patterns when the doors opened, or setting in motion the mechanism of a musical box.

12. Cigarette Cards

It is sad to think that after only seventy-odd years, this apparently inexhaustible mine of information has been worked out. What a pity it is that the last war finished them off, when the Great War tried and failed. The world may not have lost a great art form, but it has lost a lot of fun, the first stimulus to many collectors who went on to greater things and a very palatable form of acquiring knowledge.

Cigarette cards, like tobacco itself, came in the first place from America, but it was in this country that they really came into their own. Their origins were quite unromantic. In the eighteen eighties, cigarettes were sold not in the substantial cardboard packets we know today, but in flimsy paper wrappings. To keep the contents of the packet from getting crushed in the pocket, cardboard stiffeners were put in. One of the most common sizes of paper packet held five cigarettes, and the stiffeners were just big enough to cover these – about $2\frac{1}{2}'' \times 1\frac{1}{2}''$. In Britain, the first stiffeners (this was the name by which cigarette cards were known to the trade throughout their existence) were quite blank, but one authority claims that as early as 1878, illustrated stiffeners were being used in cigarette packets. One of the original firms to use them was R. P. Gloag (long since amalgamated with a larger company). It was in 1887 that one famous manufacturer (Wills) began to put a few lines of advertising material on them, followed three years later by a picture of the packet, and in 1894 by replicas of their advertising showcards. In 1895 the first English cigarette cards as we know them appeared.

This was some ten years after America, where by 1888 there were a large number of pictorial sets being produced. These early

American examples, although they had pictures and scenes in colour on the front, did not carry details of the illustration on the back. Instead, they carried advertising material, or a list of the other titles in the same series. As a rule, these early American cards were not put into the cigarette packets, but were given separately to customers who bought cigarettes. Many of the subjects were very similar to those of half a century later – Dogs of the World, Flags of the Nations and Great World Leaders, for example. Music-hall stars were popular, as were cards in the form of miniature playing cards.

The Americans had a strange habit (induced apparently by the belief that nothing helps sales along like a pretty girl) of adding

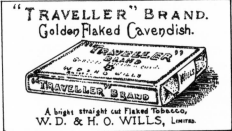

Early cigarette cards

girls' heads or bathing belles to a whole range of subjects; so one could collect Steamers (and girls), or Fishers and Fish (and girls), or Flowers (and girls). The champion set of this kind was certainly International Signals, on which flag signals in the International Code were shown in colour together with their meaning, and a picture of a girl as a quite separate decoration; prized items in this set include the signals 'I am on fire' with a particularly cool lady; and 'Let go the Buoy'.

American tobacco firms also produced before the end of the nineteenth century a larger size of card, about $4\frac{1}{2}'' \times 2\frac{1}{2}''$, for use in boxes; these did not prove to be nearly as popular as the smaller 'standard' cards, and did not last long. Other early American examples include 'folders', which opened like a small book and contained the picture inside while the outside was an imitation of the fur of various animals; sets of diamond shape; and many other fanciful and eye-catching variations.

Britain at the end of the Victorian era was in the full flush of her colonialism, and many of the early English sets had a martial or patriotic ring about them – 'Ships' issued by Wills in 1895 was one of the very earliest and it was soon followed by 'Soldiers and Sailors'. Wills, in 1901, put in their cigarette packets small enamelled brass tokens, six making up a full set, to commemorate the Boer War. These tokens were designed to be worn on a watch chain.

Our own tobacco companies never showed quite the same enthusiasm for decorative beauties as their American counterparts. One famous set, however, was devoted to girls' heads, pictured on cards which were the size and shape of tobacco leaves, and Churchmans issued a set of circular cards illustrating lovely ladies too. This set, unlike many others which appeared at intervals throughout the first fifty years of the present century, was never repeated, probably because it was found that the cost of production was too high. Another firm imported from America cards showing girls' heads, on the back of which were dominoes to make up a full set.

America soon gave up the production of cigarette cards largely because of a law that prohibited the inclusion of any other material in the packing of tobacco. Although the law was aimed at gift coupons, it effectively banished cigarette cards too; a pity, because the modern flimsy cigarette 'packs' could do with stiffeners. Britain, however, went from strength to strength and produced an enormous number of colourful, and in most cases well printed, sets between 1900 and 1917. They struggled through the first years of the Great War, producing in the process some exceptionally interesting examples of early propaganda, personalities and cartoons, until the paper shortage brought them to a temporary halt.

J. & T. Hodge of Glasgow and Illingworths both introduced 'beautiful landscape' cards for the first time in 1893; Hodges' showed Scottish scenery, Illingworths' miniatures of the Lake District. Cards were now coming in an amazing variety – educational, historical, glimpses of the future, statesmen, actors and actresses, sportsmen, animals – few things were outside their scope. Although most of them were made in the standard size of $2\frac{1}{2}" \times 1\frac{1}{2}"$, several other sizes were tried and were temporarily popular. Large standards, twice the size of the normal; postcard sizes, miniatures; long, narrow cards, with the illustration and the descriptive material side by side on the front of the card and advertising material on the back; sectional cards, to be made up into a large picture by fitting them together into a sort of jigsaw as they were collected (landscapes and famous paintings were offered in this form); cut-out figures to form an army or a football team or a corps-de-ballet.

Even stereoscopic cards were produced, with titles such as 'Peeps into Many Lands' and 'Peeps into Prehistoric Times'. The stereoscope was obtainable, at a price of course, from the manufacturers. Another popular series of the optical illusion type was 'Flickers', in which the full set, when put in the right order and the edges snapped against the thumb one after the other, produced a moving picture.

Other novelties were sets of playing cards in miniature (one manufacturer offered as an alternative to exchange four of their miniature playing cards for one full-sized one); silk flags of all the nations – beautifully produced and one of the most popular sets ever made; sets of 'Flowers' and 'Regimental Badges', also well-produced

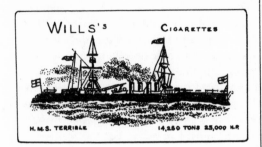

Cigarette cards with a military slant

in silk; and a series of national flags designed to be worn in the buttonhole.

Probably the longest series was issued by Ogdens between 1899 and 1910. The length of the series was helped by the sweeping title – Actresses, Prominent People and Subjects of General Interest. More than 20,000 different cards made up a complete social history of the period.

Many of the firms which issued cards with their cigarettes, and which in their day had become household words, merged with more powerful competitors, Gloag, Churchmans, Hills, Biggs, Cohen Weenan, Johnsons, William Clarke, F. & J. Smith, Franks & Sons, Robinson & Sons, H. A. C., Copes, Gabriels, Godfrey Phillips &

Sons, Morris, Adkins, Baker & Co., J. & T. Hodge, Milhoff, Illingworth – all these disappeared into the portals of better-organised or richer rivals.

Although a few sets were produced in South America, Switzerland, Spain, Italy, Norway, Portugal, Belgium, South Africa, Canada, Australia, New Zealand, Malta, the West Indies, China, Japan and India, the only other countries which produced cigarette cards in any large quantity were Germany and Egypt. Germany did not begin until after the Great War and, although her later products were modelled on those of Britain, the first German cards were made of paper rather than cardboard, and each picture was perforated like a stamp at the edges. These cards were made in large sheets and separated into individual cards only as they were inserted by hand into the packets. Some of the most interesting German cards were those of the 1930's, devoted as they were almost entirely to propaganda. Typical series were 'All for Germany' and 'Germany High in Renown'. One set agitated for the return of the German colonies, commandeered after the Great War.

German cards varied very much in size. One minor characteristic was the way in which different manufacturers would include identical cards in their products, a practice which was never followed in Britain.

Egyptian cards, which were issued in quite large numbers, were apparently devoted to three subjects only – Actresses, Beauties and Love Scenes.

Finally, in this necessarily brief survey of cigarette cards, was it true that the manufacturers would deliberately hold back one or two cards out of a set so that collectors would desperately buy extra packets of cigarettes to get the final cards? This was always indignantly denied by the makers, but even so one sometimes wondered. Whatever the ethics of it, it is quite certain that a lot of cigarettes were bought for the attractive cards inside the packet.

One strange rumour that was widely believed just before the last war was that a famous company would pay a pension for life to any crippled child whose friends collected 50,000 cards in six months from the particular company's packets. How this rumour arose (it was quite untrue) was a mystery, but it probably sold quite a lot of cigarettes as well as causing considerable embarrassment to the company concerned.

For a more detailed account of the enormous variety of cigarette cards issued, the reader is recommended to A. J. Cruse's *Cigarette Card Cavalcade* published in 1948, or I. O. Evans' *Cigarette Cards and How to Collect them* published in 1937.

THE LAST PUFF

Whether you are a smoker or not (and we have tried to avoid partiality in either direction) you will, we hope, have been entertained by this account of the bygones of tobacco. We also hope you may be stimulated to recognise some unknown piece of junk for what it is, and to rescue it. Far too many bygones are being thrown away because nobody knows what they are. Happily, there is a growing awareness of their value (in terms of heritage rather than cash), and many museums are clearing out their decaying stuffed birds and filling the space with displays of equipment that our grandfathers used. It may well be that some future generation will wonder what 'smoking' was, and will be astonished and amused by a visit to the local museum; where a collection of tobacco bygones started by you and by us will convince them that their ancestors were extremely odd people.

An Abbreviated Bibliography

Apperson, G. L.	*Social History of Smoking* (1914)
Bryant & May	*Catalogue of Museum of Fire-making Appliances* (1926)
Corti, Count	*A History of Smoking* (1931)
Cruse, A. J.	*Cigarette Card Cavalcade* (1948)
Dunhill, Alfred	*The Pipe Book* (1924)
Evans, I. O.	*Cigarette Cards and How to Collect Them* (1937)
Fairholt F. W.	*Tobacco: Its History and Associations* (1876)
Heal, Ambrose	*Signboards of Old London Shops* (1947)
Herment, G.	*The Pipe* (1954)
Jobson, A.	*Household and Country Crafts* (1953)
Larwood J. & Hotten, J. C.	*History of Signboards* (1866)
Lindsey, J. S.	*Iron and Brass Implements of the English House* (1964)
Mackenzie, Sir Compton	*Sublime Tobacco* (1957)
Massingham H. J.	*Country Relics* (1939)
Mathias, P.	*English Trade Tokens* (1962)
McCausland, H.	*Snuff and Snuff Boxes* (1951)
Meadows, Cecil A.	*Tradesigns and Their Origin* (1957)
Myer, Reginald	*Chats on Old English Tobacco Jars* (1927)
O'Dea, W. T.	*Making Fire* (1964)
Penn, W. A.	*The Soverane Herbe* (1901)
Pinto, Edward H.	*Treen* (1949)
Pinto, Edward H.	*Wooden Bygones of Smoking and Snuff Taking* (1961)
Rendell, J.	*Collecting Matchbox Labels* (1963)
Scott, Amoret & Christopher	*Collecting Bygones* (1964)
Tennant, R. B.	*The American Cigarette Industry* (1950)

INDEX

A

Ashtrays 147

B

Brass Tobacco Boxes 68
Brass Tobacco Jars 68
Burning Glasses 83

C

Chinese Pipes 42
Chinese Snuff Bottles 124
Cigars 148
Cigar Cases 150
Cigar Cutters 157
Cigar Dispensers 153
Cigar Holders 154
Cigar Labels 138
Cigar Mould 156
Cigar-smoking Companion 157
Cigar Tips and Caps 88
Cigarettes 159
Cigarette Cards 167
Cigarette Cases 165
Cigarette Holders 162
Cigarette-making Machines 163
Cigarette Stands 166
Congreves 89
Clay Pipe-making Tools 49
Clay Pipes 24

D

Dress 139

E

Electro-Pneumatic Lamps 84
Enamelled Snuff-boxes 117
Eskimo Pipes 42

F

Fire Pistons 80
Friction Matches 86
Furniture 139
Fuzees 87

G

Glass Pipes 38
Gold Snuff-boxes 114

H

Horn Snuff-boxes 122

I

Instantaneous Light Contrivances 81
Ivory Snuff-boxes 115

J

Japanese Pipes 42

L

Laurencekirk Boxes 119
Lead Tobacco Jars 59
Lighters 94

M

Match Containers 91
Matchbox Labels 99
Mechanical Boxes 69
Mechanical Tinder Boxes 79
Meerschaum Pipes 32
Mould Pipes 40

P

Paper Ephemera 136
Papier Mâché Snuff-boxes 121
Pewter Tobacco Jars 65
Pipes 24–43
Pipe Burners 44
Pipe-burning Rack 45
Pipe Cases 51
Pipe Kiln 45
Pipe of Peace 41
Pipe Racks 48
Pocket Snuff-rasps 110
Pocket Tinder Boxes 76
Porcelain Pipes 35
Porcelain Snuff-boxes 117
Pottery Pipes 37
Pottery Tobacco Jars 66
Promethean Matches 86

S

Silver Snuff-boxes 116
Smokers' Chairs 144
Smoking Caps 141
Smoking Jackets 140
Snuff 109
Snuff-boxes 114–122
Snuff Handkerchiefs 142
Snuff-mulls 122

Snuff Waistcoats 142
Special Box, A 70
Spill Vases 145
Spillcutters 146
Spittoons 143
Steel Tobacco Boxes 69
Steels 73
Sulphur Matches 77

T

Tinder Boxes 75
Tinder Horns 76
Tinder Pistols 79
Tinder Pouches 76
Tobacco Boxes 68–71
Tobacco Cutters 56
Tobacco Jars 59–68
Tobacco Pouches 141
Tobacco Prickers 56
Tobacco Stoppers 53
Tobacco Tongs 46
Tortoiseshell Snuff-boxes 115
Trade Signs 126
Trade Tokens 133
Tube Pipes 40

V

Vesuvians 89

W

Water Pipes 42
Wooden Pipes 39
Wooden Snuff-boxes 118
Wooden Tobacco Jars 65